ISBN: 0-9826608-0-4
ISBN 13: 978-0-9826608-0-5

You can visit us online at: **www.JacKrisPublishing.com**

Copyright 2010 by JacKris Publishing, LLC. All rights reserved. No part of this publication may be reproduced or transmitted in any form or by any means, electronic or mechanical, including photocopying, recording, or any information storage and/or retrieval system or device, without permission in writing from the publisher or as authorized by United States Copyright Law.

Printed in the United States of America.

Ver. 1.0.0-1

Copyright 2010 Soaring with Spelling and Vocabulary Level 7. All Rights Reserved.

Preface

We have designed this thorough program to be user friendly for both teacher and student. The **level 7** program consists of this workbook and the **Teacher's Notes/Answer key**.

At the beginning of the workbook is a table of contents that lists the concepts and the lessons that pertain to each.

We have selected spiral binding for our books to ensure that they lie flat when open. The spiral binding at the top of the page provides equal, unobstructed access for both right and left-handed students.

Thank you for choosing **Soaring with Spelling and Vocabulary**. We look forward to the opportunity to provide you with the best tools possible to educate your children.

How To Use This Program

This program is arranged in 36 weekly lessons. Each lesson consists of five exercises labeled **Day 1** through **Day 5**.

For the level 7 program we have selected eighteen list words for each week (for each lesson). Eighteen new words each week should provide an adequate challenge for a student at this level. The list words are meant to provide the student with an introduction to one new spelling concept each week. By gently introducing each new concept, one at a time, the student should not become overwhelmed.

We have found that most children in the age group for which these materials are designed usually need to spend about 10-15 minutes per day on spelling and vocabulary. If your student happens to progress through the material at a faster rate, you may want to consider condensing each lesson into a four day schedule. This can be accomplished in a number of ways, such as combining **Day 1** and **Day 2**, or perhaps combining **Day 4** and **Day 5**. It's really up to you as long as all of the materials are covered during each week.

Please see the **Teacher's Notes/Answer Key** for a detailed explanation (which includes a recommended **Weekly Schedule**) on how to use these materials.

Copyright 2010 Soaring with Spelling and Vocabulary Level 7. All Rights Reserved.

Level 7

Table of Contents

Lesson 1 – Words with **cher** and **zher** sounds... 1

Lesson 2 – Words with vowel and consonant digraphs... 7

Lesson 3 – Words with double consonants.. 13

Lesson 4 – Adding **er** and **est** to words that end in **y**... 19

Lesson 5 – Words with **Greek** and **Latin prefixes** and **suffixes**.............................. 25

    Lesson 6 – Review of lessons 1–5... 31

Lesson 7 – Words with **cian**, **tion**, and **sion**.. 37

Lesson 8 – Words with **able**, **ible**, and **ous**... 43

Lesson 9 – Words with **under**... 49

Lesson 10 – Words with the **schwa** sound... 55

Lesson 11 – Words with the **f** sound using **f**, **ff**, **ph**, and **gh**................................... 61

    Lesson 12 – Review of lessons 7-11... 67

Lesson 13 – Words with **geo**, **act**, **bio**, **port**, and **graph**.. 73

Lesson 14 – Words that mean a type of **sound** made with the mouth........................ 79

Lesson 15 – Words with prefixes **mis** and **anti**.. 85

Lesson 16 – Words with **con** and **non**... 91

Lesson 17 – Words that mean **to move**.. 97

    Lesson 18 – Review of lessons 13-17... 103

Lesson 19 – Words that have to do with **feelings** or **emotions**................................ 109

Lesson 20 – Words with **ar**, **are**, **or**, and **ore**... 115

Lesson 21 – Words with **tch** and **sch**... 121

Copyright 2010 Soaring with Spelling and Vocabulary Level 7. All Rights Reserved.

Lesson 22 – Words that begin with **bene**, **bon**, and **boun**............................ 127

Lesson 23 – Words with consonant blends **cl** and **cr**.................................. 133

    Lesson 24 – Reviews of lessons 19-23.. 139

Lesson 25 – Words with silent letters.. 145

Lesson 26 – Easily misspelled words.. 151

Lesson 27 – Words with different **s** sounds...................................... 157

Lesson 28 – Words with **over** and **out**.. 163

Lesson 29 – Words with **ei** and **ie**.. 169

    Lesson 30 – Review of lessons 25-29.. 175

Lesson 31 – Four-syllable words.. 181

Lesson 32 – Words with prefixes **uni**, **mono**, **bi**, **tri**, and **mid**.................. 187

Lesson 33 – Words with **sub**, **ultra**, and **dia**.................................. 193

Lesson 34 – Words with **counter** and **super**.................................... 199

Lesson 35 – Words that begin with **consonant blends**.............................. 205

    Lesson 36 – Review of lessons 31-35.. 211

Copyright 2010 Soaring with Spelling and Vocabulary Level 7. All Rights Reserved.

Student's Name: _____

Soaring with Spelling and Vocabulary

Level 7

Copyright 2010 Soaring with Spelling and Vocabulary Level 7. All Rights Reserved.

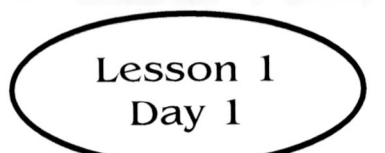

Date: _____

Words with **cher** and **zher** sounds

1. **Review Your List Words**
   Look at the list words below and read each word to yourself. Then review each definition.

List Words/Definitions

pasture *pasture*	closure *closure*
• A grassy land upon which animals feed.	• The act of closing or bringing something to an end.
temperature *temperature*	disclosure *disclosure*
• The measurement of hotness or coldness.	• The act of making something known.
structure *structure*	composure *composure*
• Something that is built or constructed.	• To appear calm.
measure *measure*	furniture *furniture*
• Extent or amount.	• Movable items within a house that can be sat on or used to store items.
pleasure *pleasure*	capture *capture*
• A feeling of enjoyment.	• To take and hold by force.
feature *feature*	mixture *mixture*
• The main attraction. Also, a main story in a newspaper or magazine.	• To blend two or more ingredients.
literature *literature*	culture *culture*
• Written material such as poetry, novels, or essays.	• Traits related to a civilization.
creature *creature*	fracture *fracture*
• A living being. Especially an animal.	• A break of something.
treasure *treasure*	leisure *leisure*
• Money or jewels of great wealth.	• Time of rest or freedom.

2. **Take Your Pretest**
   Turn to the next page to the Pretest section and your teacher will ask you to write each list word one at a time.

Date: _____

Pretest - Lesson 1:   Correction Area:

1. _____   _____
2. _____   _____
3. _____   _____
4. _____   _____
5. _____   _____
6. _____   _____
7. _____   _____
8. _____   _____
9. _____   _____
10. _____   _____
11. _____   _____
12. _____   _____
13. _____   _____
14. _____   _____
15. _____   _____
16. _____   _____
17. _____   _____
18. _____   _____

Level 7, Lesson 1 – Words with **cher** and **zher** sounds

Lesson 1 Day 2

Date: _____

pasture	pleasure	closure	mixture
temperature	feature	disclosure	culture
structure	literature	composure	fracture
measure	creature	furniture	leisure
	treasure	capture	

A. Finish each list word. Use each list word only once.

1. pa_____
2. t____m_____
3. tr_____
4. ca_____
5. s_____
6. ___ei_____
7. ____x_____
8. cr_____
9. c_____po_____
10. fe_____
11. pl_____
12. ___ur_____
13. me_____
14. fr_____
15. li_____
16. cl_____
17. cu_____
18. d_____

B. Copy the following sentences. **Jerry received a leg fracture during his leisure trip to learn about the culture of Japan.**

_____
_____
_____
_____
_____

C. Write the definition from Day 1 for the list word **closure**.

_____
_____
_____

Level 7, Lesson 1 – Words with **cher** and **zher** sounds

Date: _____

Lesson 1 Day 3

pasture	pleasure	closure	mixture
temperature	feature	disclosure	culture
structure	literature	composure	fracture
measure	creature	furniture	leisure
	treasure	capture	

A. Read the following sentences and write on the lines below the list words you see.

   The pasture with the barn structure, that held the creature that we had to capture, had a buried treasure according to the disclosure made in the feature of the literature on *Lost Treasures*.

1. _____   2. _____

3. _____   4. _____

5. _____   6. _____

7. _____   8. _____

   It was a pleasure for Jared to measure the temperature of the cake mixture of eggs and flour in the bowl on the shelf. He nearly lost his composure when he received a finger fracture when he fell trying to reach the bowl.

9. _____   10. _____

11. _____   12. _____

13. _____   14. _____

   It was the culture within our furniture business to attain closure on all pending work before leaving to spend leisure time on vacation.

15. _____   16. _____

17. _____   18. _____

B. Copy the following sentences. **The farmer wanted to measure the space within the structure that used to be located in the pasture.**

_____

_____

_____

_____

Level 7, Lesson 1 – Words with **cher** and **zher** sounds

Date: _____

Lesson 1 Day 4

pasture	pleasure	closure	mixture
temperature	feature	disclosure	culture
structure	literature	composure	fracture
measure	creature	furniture	leisure
	treasure	capture	

A. Underline the list word in each group that is spelled correctly.

1. treasure	tresure	treazure
2. capcher	capture	captuir
3. leasure	leesure	leisure
4. temperture	temperature	termpiture
5. creatire	creacher	creature
6. furniture	furnichure	furnituire
7. mixchure	mixture	mixtcher
8. mesure	measur	measure
9. pastcher	pasture	pasther
10. plessure	pleasure	pleasur
11. composure	composur	composuire
12. fractuir	fracture	fractur
13. culture	culcher	culraine
14. disclosure	discloshir	disclosur
15. closhure	closure	clothsure
16. feature	feeture	featshur
17. structure	strucshur	structsher
18. litrature	literature	literatur

B. Write a short paragraph below using at least four list words.

_____

_____

_____

_____

_____

_____

Level 7, Lesson 1 – Words with **cher** and **zher** sounds

5

Lesson 1 - Day 5, Final Test

Date: _____

Correction Area:

1. _____ _____
2. _____ _____
3. _____ _____
4. _____ _____
5. _____ _____
6. _____ _____
7. _____ _____
8. _____ _____
9. _____ _____
10. _____ _____
11. _____ _____
12. _____ _____
13. _____ _____
14. _____ _____
15. _____ _____
16. _____ _____
17. _____ _____
18. _____ _____

Carry-over Words: Correction Area:

1. _____ _____
2. _____ _____
3. _____ _____
4. _____ _____

Level 7, Lesson 1 – Words with **cher** and **zher** sounds

Words with **vowel** and consonant digraphs

1. **Review Your List Words**
   Look at the list words below and read each word to yourself. Then review each definition.

   A **digraph** is two letters placed side by side that act together to make one sound. For example, the letters **ey** in the word **k<u>ey</u>board** makes a long **e** sound and the letters **ck** in the word **aftersho<u>ck</u>** make a **k** sound.

   Consonant digraphs: **ck, ng, wh, sh, ch, pr, scr,** and **qu**
   Vowel digraphs: **ee, ey, ay, ai, oo, oa, ou, ue, au,** and **aw**

   The **digraphs** have been underlined in each list word below.

   ## List Words/Definitions

k<u>ey</u>board *keyboard* • A row of keys on a device that can be pressed.	**<u>sh</u>out** *shout* • A sudden loud cry.
aftersho<u>ck</u> *aftershock* • Smaller movement of the earth's crust after an earthquake.	**whirlp<u>oo</u>l** *whirlpool* • A rapidly rotating current of water.
barg<u>ai</u>n *bargain* • An agreement between parties. Also, a discount purchase.	**f<u>ee</u>dback** *feedback* • A response to an action or statement.
pl<u>ay</u>book *playbook* • A collection of strategic plans to win a contest.	**gues<u>th</u>ouse** *guesthouse* • A separate dwelling where visitors stay during a visit.
<u>scr</u>eenplay *screenplay* • A script that has been adapted for a motion picture film.	**<u>qu</u>en<u>ch</u>** *quench* • To end something by satisfying the need.
airb<u>oa</u>t *airboat* • A boat that skims the water and is driven by a propeller moving air.	**prolo<u>ng</u>** *prolong* • To make something take longer than normal.
<u>ch</u>ains<u>aw</u> *chainsaw* • A mechanized tool used to cut lumber.	**bookk<u>ee</u>per** *bookkeeper* • One who keeps financial records for a business.
al<u>th</u><u>ou</u>gh *although* • In spite of something.	**<u>wh</u>a<u>ck</u>** *whack* • A hard, swift blow.
<u>au</u><u>th</u>or *author* • Someone who writes a literary work.	**ang<u>ui</u><u>sh</u>** *anguish* • Great trouble or pain

2. **Take Your Pretest**
   Turn to the next page to the Pretest section and your teacher will ask you to write each list word one at a time.

Date: _____

Pretest - Lesson 2: **Correction Area:**

1. _____ _____
2. _____ _____
3. _____ _____
4. _____ _____
5. _____ _____
6. _____ _____
7. _____ _____
8. _____ _____
9. _____ _____
10. _____ _____
11. _____ _____
12. _____ _____
13. _____ _____
14. _____ _____
15. _____ _____
16. _____ _____
17. _____ _____
18. _____ _____

Carry-over Words: **Correction Area:**

1. _____ _____
2. _____ _____
3. _____ _____
4. _____ _____

Level 7, Lesson 2 – Words with vowel and consonant digraphs

Lesson 2 Day 2

Date: _____

keyboard	screenplay	shout	prolong
aftershock	airboat	whirlpool	bookkeeper
bargain	chainsaw	feedback	whack
playbook	although	guesthouse	anguish
	author	quench	

A. Cross out the word that is spelled incorrectly. Write the correctly spelled words on the lines.

1. (keybored, keyboard) _____
2. (plaiybook, playbook) _____
3. (awthur, author) _____
4. (quench, qench) _____
5. (anguishe, anguish) _____
6. (bookeeper, bookkeeper) _____
7. (whack, wack) _____
8. (prolone, prolong) _____
9. (geisthouse, guesthouse) _____
10. (bargain, bargan) _____
11. (althogh, although) _____
12. (fedeback, feedback) _____
13. (showte, shout) _____
14. (screenplay, screneplay) _____
15. (aftershok, aftershock) _____
16. (aireboat, airboat) _____
17. (wirlpool, whirlpool) _____
18. (chainsaw, chanesaw) _____

B. Copy the following sentence. **Although the bookkeeper preferred to use a keyboard to write the screenplay, she used paper and pencil.**

_____

_____

_____

Level 7, Lesson 2 – Words with vowel and consonant digraphs

Date: _____

Lesson 2 Day 3

keyboard	screenplay	shout	prolong
aftershock	airboat	whirlpool	bookkeeper
bargain	chainsaw	feedback	whack
playbook	although	guesthouse	anguish
	author	quench	

A. Match the list word with its definition. Draw a line to connect each pair.

keyboard	In spite of something.
screenplay	A hard swift blow.
shout	Great trouble or pain.
prolong	Someone who writes a literary work.
bookkeeper	One who keeps financial records for a business.
whirlpool	A mechanized tool used to cut lumber.
airboat	To make something take longer than normal.
aftershock	A boat that skims the water and is driven by a propeller moving air.
bargain	To end something by satisfying the need.
chainsaw	A script adapted for a motion picture film.
feedback	A separate dwelling where visitors stay.
whack	A collection of strategic plans to win a contest.
playbook	A response to an action or statement.
although	An agreement between parties.
guesthouse	Smaller movement of the earth's crust.
anguish	A sudden loud cry.
author	A rapidly rotating current of water.
quench	A row of keys on a device that can be pressed.

B. Write the definition from Day 1 for the list word **chainsaw**.

_____

_____

_____

Level 7, Lesson 2 – Words with vowel and consonant digraphs

Date: _____

keyboard	screenplay	shout	prolong
aftershock	airboat	whirlpool	bookkeeper
bargain	chainsaw	feedback	whack
playbook	although	guesthouse	anguish
	author	quench	

A. Underline the digraphs in each list word. Then write the letters that form each digraph on the line. Some list words may have more than one digraph.

1. keyboard   _____
2. playbook   _____
3. author   _____
4. quench   _____
5. anguish   _____
6. bookkeeper   _____
7. whack   _____
8. prolong   _____
9. guesthouse   _____
10. bargain   _____
11. although   _____
12. feedback   _____
13. shout   _____
14. screenplay   _____
15. aftershock   _____
16. airboat   _____
17. whirlpool   _____
18. chainsaw   _____

B. Write the definition from Day 1 for the list word **guesthouse**.

_____

_____

_____

Level 7, Lesson 2 – Words with vowel and consonant digraphs

Date: _____

Lesson 2 - Day 5, Final Test: Correction Area:

1. _____ _____
2. _____ _____
3. _____ _____
4. _____ _____
5. _____ _____
6. _____ _____
7. _____ _____
8. _____ _____
9. _____ _____
10. _____ _____
11. _____ _____
12. _____ _____
13. _____ _____
14. _____ _____
15. _____ _____
16. _____ _____
17. _____ _____
18. _____ _____

Carry-over Words: Correction Area:

1. _____ _____
2. _____ _____
3. _____ _____
4. _____ _____

Level 7, Lesson 2 – Words with vowel and consonant digraphs

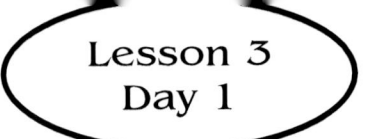

Lesson 3 Day 1

Words with double consonants

1. **Review Your List Words**
Look at the list words below and read each word to yourself. Then review each definition.

List Words/Definitions

beginning *beginning*	illegible *illegible*
• The starting point of something.	• Not readable.
anniversary *anniversary*	**hallucinate** *hallucinate*
• A date that signifies an important event.	• Seeing or thinking something that is not real.
announcement *announcement*	**suppress** *suppress*
• A public statement.	• To be held or put down by force.
accessory *accessory*	**peppermint** *peppermint*
• Something that is used to assist something else.	• A sweet, minty-tasting flavor that is often used in candy.
fortress *fortress*	**opportunity** *opportunity*
• A reinforced or fortified place.	• A chance that presents itself that will allow one to better himself.
stepladder *stepladder*	**forgotten** *forgotten*
• A small portable ladder.	• Unremembered. Left behind.
suddenly *suddenly*	**spaghetti** *spaghetti*
• Happening without warning.	• A long, stringy, noodle that is eaten with a red sauce.
downtrodden *downtrodden*	**correction** *correction*
• Those who are abused or oppressed by people in a position of authority.	• The fixing of a mistake.
allegation *allegation*	**embarrass** *embarrass*
• An accusation without actual proof.	• To be distressed by an uncomfortable surprise.

2. **Take Your Pretest**
Turn to the next page to the Pretest section and your teacher will ask you to write each list word one at a time.

Date: _____

Pretest - Lesson 3:

1. _____
2. _____
3. _____
4. _____
5. _____
6. _____
7. _____
8. _____
9. _____
10. _____
11. _____
12. _____
13. _____
14. _____
15. _____
16. _____
17. _____
18. _____

Correction Area:

_____
_____
_____
_____
_____
_____
_____
_____
_____
_____
_____
_____
_____
_____
_____
_____
_____
_____

Carry-over Words:

1. _____
2. _____
3. _____
4. _____

Correction Area:

_____
_____
_____
_____

Level 7, Lesson 3 – Words with double consonants

Date: _____

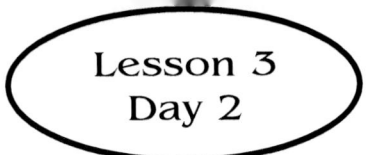

Lesson 3 Day 2

beginning	fortress	illegible	forgotten
anniversary	stepladder	hallucinate	spaghetti
announcement	suddenly	suppress	correction
accessory	downtrodden	peppermint	embarrass
	allegation	opportunity	

A. Find and circle each list word in the puzzle below.

```
T  D  Y  S  B  E  T  Y  O  H  Y  T  J  A  Y  H  S  T  C  K
Z  N  O  T  F  Z  T  H  N  R  P  V  C  P  L  G  P  N  B  T
E  S  I  W  G  F  G  D  A  P  Y  C  Z  H  N  Z  A  E  J  M
Y  Z  S  M  N  P  D  S  H  I  E  V  D  I  E  H  G  M  K  R
N  N  S  E  R  T  R  T  I  S  M  F  N  L  D  B  H  E  Z  T
B  S  U  F  R  E  R  C  S  N  U  N  M  X  D  H  E  C  W  Z
L  C  S  D  V  T  P  O  I  T  I  F  O  N  U  K  T  N  F  A
Q  L  L  I  X  T  R  P  D  G  H  R  P  O  S  Z  T  U  F  F
G  I  N  I  E  Y  N  O  E  D  F  A  P  I  Y  A  I  O  U  C
I  N  N  S  M  B  T  B  F  P  E  O  O  T  T  E  Q  N  M  O
A  I  L  L  E  G  I  B  L  E  A  N  R  A  R  S  X  N  A  S
O  M  N  T  Y  Z  Q  B  O  V  A  Z  T  G  O  U  L  A  T  A
U  L  Y  O  J  H  S  O  T  E  C  N  U  E  O  T  U  E  W  S
N  O  I  T  C  E  R  R  O  C  S  X  N  L  M  T  P  T  S  O
S  S  A  R  R  A  B  M  E  E  J  C  I  L  L  L  T  E  V  S
C  H  A  L  L  U  C  I  N  A  T  E  T  A  A  N  R  E  Q  L
V  B  D  X  X  U  I  C  D  T  Q  Y  Y  D  S  P  B  Y  N  U
H  F  A  I  R  N  F  Q  I  W  G  N  D  U  P  O  M  B  L  P
F  N  O  E  G  I  O  G  A  K  L  E  O  U  N  V  T  X  S  Q
I  N  I  W  V  S  O  V  B  Z  R  J  S  W  W  C  T  A  Y  O
```

Level 7, Lesson 3 – Words with double consonants

Date: _____

Lesson 3
Day 3

beginning	fortress	illegible	forgotten
anniversary	stepladder	hallucinate	spaghetti
announcement	suddenly	suppress	correction
accessory	downtrodden	peppermint	embarrass
	allegation	opportunity	

A. **Guide words** are placed at the top of each page of a dictionary to provide an alphabetical guide for finding entry words that appear on that page. For example, assume that a page has the guide words **fast** and **feline**. The entry word **farmer** would **not** be found on that page because alphabetically it does not fall between these guide words. On the other hand, the entry word **feeling** would be found on that page.

Look at each pair of guide words, then write the list word on the line that would appear on the dictionary page.

1. annex   announce   _____
2. anniversary   annoy   _____
3. accept   accident   _____
4. embargo   ember   _____
5. corral   corrupt   _____
6. beg   behalf   _____
7. all   allergic   _____
8. doubt   draft   _____
9. forge   fork   _____
10. fortitude   fortunate   _____
11. ill   illusion   _____
12. stencil   stereo   _____
13. such   sue   _____
14. supply   surf   _____
15. spade   span   _____
16. people   per   _____
17. hall   halt   _____
18. opinion   optic   _____

Level 7, Lesson 3 – Words with double consonants

Date: _____

Lesson 3 Day 4

beginning	fortress	illegible	forgotten
anniversary	stepladder	hallucinate	spaghetti
announcement	suddenly	suppress	correction
accessory	downtrodden	peppermint	embarrass
	allegation	opportunity	

A. Cross out the word that is spelled incorrectly.

1. (begining, beginning)
2. (allegation allagation)
3. (oportunity, opportunity)
4. (embarras, embarrass)
5. (correction, correctiun)
6. (accesory, accessory)
7. (aniversary, anniversary)
8. (fourtress, fortress)
9. (suddenly, suddenlie)
10. (spagetti, spaghetti)
11. (downtrodden, downtroden)
12. (steplatter, stepladder)
13. (ilegible, illegible)
14. (forgottan, forgotten)
15. (announcement, announcemunt)
16. (supress, suppress)
17. (halucinate, hallucinate)
18. (peppermint, pepermint)

B. Write a short paragraph below using at least four list words.

_____
_____
_____
_____
_____

C. Copy the following sentence. **Stan had suddenly forgotten that the stepladder was not tall enough to climb the wall of the fortress.**

_____
_____
_____
_____

Level 7, Lesson 3 – Words with double consonants

17

Date: _____

Lesson 3 - Day 5, Final Test   Correction Area:

1. _____   _____
2. _____   _____
3. _____   _____
4. _____   _____
5. _____   _____
6. _____   _____
7. _____   _____
8. _____   _____
9. _____   _____
10. _____   _____
11. _____   _____
12. _____   _____
13. _____   _____
14. _____   _____
15. _____   _____
16. _____   _____
17. _____   _____
18. _____   _____

Carry-over Words: Correction Area:

1. _____   _____
2. _____   _____
3. _____   _____
4. _____   _____

Level 7, Lesson 3 – Words with double consonants

Lesson 4 Day 1

Adding er and est to words that end in y

1. **Review Your List Words**
   Look at the list words below and read each word to yourself. Then review each definition.

   There are a few rules to follow when adding an ending to words that end with **y**.

   -When **y** follows a **vowel**, you add **er** without changing the spelling of the base word.
   employ + er = employer

   -When **y** follows a **consonant**, you change the **y** to **i** and add **er** or **est**.
   healthy + er = healthier   scary + est = scariest

   ### List Words/Definitions

employer *employer*	scariest *scariest*
• One who hires/employs people.	• To be the most frightening.
destroyer *destroyer*	tiniest *tiniest*
• One who does away with or puts an end to something.	• To be the smallest.
sprayer *sprayer*	laziest *laziest*
• Something that scatters droplets of liquid.	• To be the most sluggish or slowest.
annoyer *annoyer*	busiest *busiest*
• One who irritates or disturbs.	• To be the most occupied or most engaged in activity.
buyer *buyer*	sleepiest *sleepiest*
• One who purchases.	• To be more tired than all the others.
healthier *healthier*	easiest *easiest*
• To be more free of disease than something else.	• To require the least amount of effort than all the others.
handier *handier*	friendliest *friendliest*
• To be more skilled than someone else in repairing or constructing something.	• To be the one who shows the most liking, goodwill, or trust.
greedier *greedier*	loveliest *loveliest*
• To have more of an excessive desire than someone else for something.	• To be the most beautiful.
carrier *carrier*	craziest *craziest*
• Something that carries something else.	• To be more mentally unstable than all the others.

2. **Take Your Pretest**
   Turn to the next page to the Pretest section and your teacher will ask you to write each list word one at a time.

Level 7, Lesson 4 – Adding **er** and **est** to words that end in **y**

Date: _____

Pretest - Lesson 4: **Correction Area:**

1. _____ _____
2. _____ _____
3. _____ _____
4. _____ _____
5. _____ _____
6. _____ _____
7. _____ _____
8. _____ _____
9. _____ _____
10. _____ _____
11. _____ _____
12. _____ _____
13. _____ _____
14. _____ _____
15. _____ _____
16. _____ _____
17. _____ _____
18. _____ _____

Carry-over Words: **Correction Area:**

1. _____ _____
2. _____ _____
3. _____ _____
4. _____ _____

Level 7, Lesson 4 – Adding **er** and **est** to words that end in **y**

Date: _____

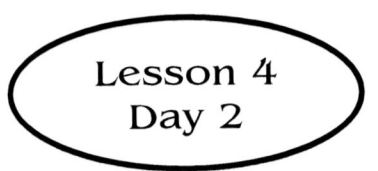

Lesson 4 Day 2

employer	buyer	scariest	easiest
destroyer	healthier	tiniest	friendliest
sprayer	handier	laziest	loveliest
annoyer	greedier	busiest	craziest
	carrier	sleepiest	

A. Find and circle each list word in the puzzle below.

```
G  F  T  E  R  R  I  T  H  R  M  E  R  D  C
O  R  M  S  N  E  S  R  E  L  A  W  E  B  R
X  I  E  O  E  E  Y  Y  E  S  T  S  I  U  A
A  E  Q  E  I  I  O  A  I  M  T  T  D  S  Z
E  N  Z  Z  D  L  L  E  R  R  L  S  N  I  I
H  D  A  J  P  I  S  E  O  P  R  E  A  E  E
U  L  J  M  D  T  E  Y  V  Q  S  I  H  S  S
O  I  E  G  Y  B  E  R  V  O  R  P  H  T  T
U  E  S  C  A  R  I  E  S  T  L  E  B  S  D
T  S  E  I  N  I  T  R  E  F  K  E  Y  Z  E
P  T  R  E  I  H  T  L  A  E  H  L  L  U  S
A  N  N  O  Y  E  R  Z  N  N  X  S  D  G  B
R  E  I  R  R  A  C  J  S  Z  Z  O  J  U  Q
O  L  M  X  W  N  E  E  K  C  J  H  B  J  B
B  S  W  K  H  F  Z  J  Y  A  P  W  Q  N  J
```

B. Copy the following sentences. **Sandy placed the tiniest sprayer of water into the carrier so she could have it at the amusement park.**

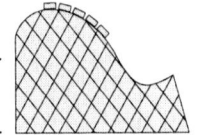

_____

_____

_____

_____

Level 7, Lesson 4 – Adding **er** and **est** to words that end in **y**

21

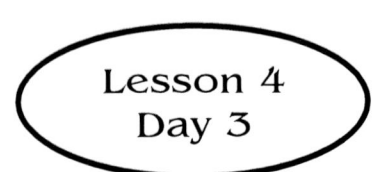

Lesson 4 Day 3

Date: _____

employer	buyer	scariest	easiest
destroyer	healthier	tiniest	friendliest
sprayer	handier	laziest	loveliest
annoyer	greedier	busiest	craziest
	carrier	sleepiest	

A. Write each group of three list words in alphabetical order.

craziest, carrier, easiest

1. _____ 2. _____ 3. _____

handier, friendliest, healthier

4. _____ 5. _____ 6. _____

buyer, busiest, annoyer

7. _____ 8. _____ 9. _____

sleepiest, scariest, sprayer

10. _____ 11. _____ 12. _____

loveliest, laziest, tiniest

13. _____ 14. _____ 15. _____

destroyer, employer, greedier

16. _____ 17. _____ 18. _____

sleepiest, scariest, loveliest

19. _____ 20. _____ 21. _____

craziest, busiest, sprayer

22. _____ 23. _____ 24. _____

tiniest, carrier, annoyer

25. _____ 26. _____ 27. _____

easiest, sprayer, employer

28. _____ 29. _____ 30. _____

Level 7, Lesson 4 – Adding **er** and **est** to words that end in **y**

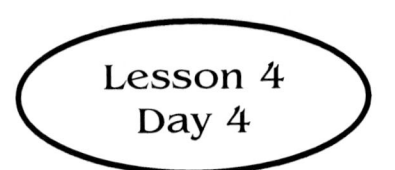

Lesson 4 Day 4

employer	buyer	scariest	easiest
destroyer	healthier	tiniest	friendliest
sprayer	handier	laziest	loveliest
annoyer	greedier	busiest	craziest
	carrier	sleepiest	

A. Finish each list word. Use each word only once.

1. d_____
2. b_____r
3. ___nn_____
4. he_____
5. ___le_____
6. h___n_____
7. c_____z_____
8. ___m_____
9. sp_____
10. sc_____
11. ___ar_____
12. l_____
13. ___as_____
14. ___us_____
15. l___z_____
16. f_____
17. t_____
18. _____ed_____

B. Copy the following sentence. **It was easiest for the buyer to be the friendliest person in the meeting even though it was not going well.**

_____

_____

_____

_____

_____

C. Write the definition from Day 1 for the list word **greedier**.

_____

_____

Level 7, Lesson 4 – Adding **er** and **est** to words that end in **y**

Date: _____

Lesson 4 - Day 5, Final Test   Correction Area:

1. _____   _____
2. _____   _____
3. _____   _____
4. _____   _____
5. _____   _____
6. _____   _____
7. _____   _____
8. _____   _____
9. _____   _____
10. _____   _____
11. _____   _____
12. _____   _____
13. _____   _____
14. _____   _____
15. _____   _____
16. _____   _____
17. _____   _____
18. _____   _____

Carry-over Words: Correction Area:

1. _____   _____
2. _____   _____
3. _____   _____
4. _____   _____

Level 7, Lesson 4 – Adding **er** and **est** to words that end in **y**

Date: _____

Words with **Greek** and **Latin** prefixes and suffixes

1. **Review Your List Words**
Look at the list words below and read each word to yourself. Then review each definition.

Below is a list of the **Greek** and **Latin prefixes** and **suffixes** used in this lesson along with their meanings.

para = beside	**facture** = make	**dict** = speak	**script/scribe** = write
pus = foot	**dia** = across	**con** = together	**octo** = eight
uni = one	**son** = sound	**scious** = know	**thesis** = put, place
manu = hand	**thermo** = heat	**pathy** = feeling	**syn/sym** = together
fix = attach	**gon** = angle	**pre** = before	**meter** = measure

List Words/Definitions

parenthesis *parenthesis* • An independent word or phrase placed into written material used to explain.	**sympathy** *sympathy* • To share the feelings of another.
symmetry *symmetry* • A measured balance among the parts of something.	**conscious** *conscious* • Aware of oneself and one's surroundings.
synthesis *synthesis* • To put together separate elements to form a whole.	**prefix** *prefix* • Letters attached to the beginning of a word. To put before or in front of.
manufacture *manufacture* • To make by hand.	**octopus** *octopus* • A marine animal that has eight legs.
manuscript *manuscript* • A document written by hand.	**unison** *unison* • The same musical pitch sung by more than one.
diameter *diameter* • The distance across a circle.	**diagonal** *diagonal* • An oblique line.
thermometer *thermometer* • A utensil used to measure temperature.	**octagon** *octagon* • A figure with eight sides and eight angles.
predict *predict* • To tell about something before it happens.	**prescribe** *prescribe* • To issue written orders for.
manual *manual* • To do something with hands.	**dictate** *dictate* • To say something with authority.

2. **Take Your Pretest**
Turn to the next page to the Pretest section and your teacher will ask you to write each list word one at a time.

Date: _____

Pretest - Lesson 5:

Correction Area:

1. _____   _____
2. _____   _____
3. _____   _____
4. _____   _____
5. _____   _____
6. _____   _____
7. _____   _____
8. _____   _____
9. _____   _____
10. _____ _____
11. _____ _____
12. _____ _____
13. _____ _____
14. _____ _____
15. _____ _____
16. _____ _____
17. _____ _____
18. _____ _____

Carry-over Words:

Correction Area:

1. _____   _____
2. _____   _____
3. _____   _____
4. _____   _____

Lesson 5 Day 2

parenthesis	manuscript	sympathy	diagonal
symmetry	diameter	conscious	octagon
synthesis	thermometer	prefix	prescribe
manufacture	predict	octopus	dictate
	manual	unison	

A. Finish the crossword puzzle.

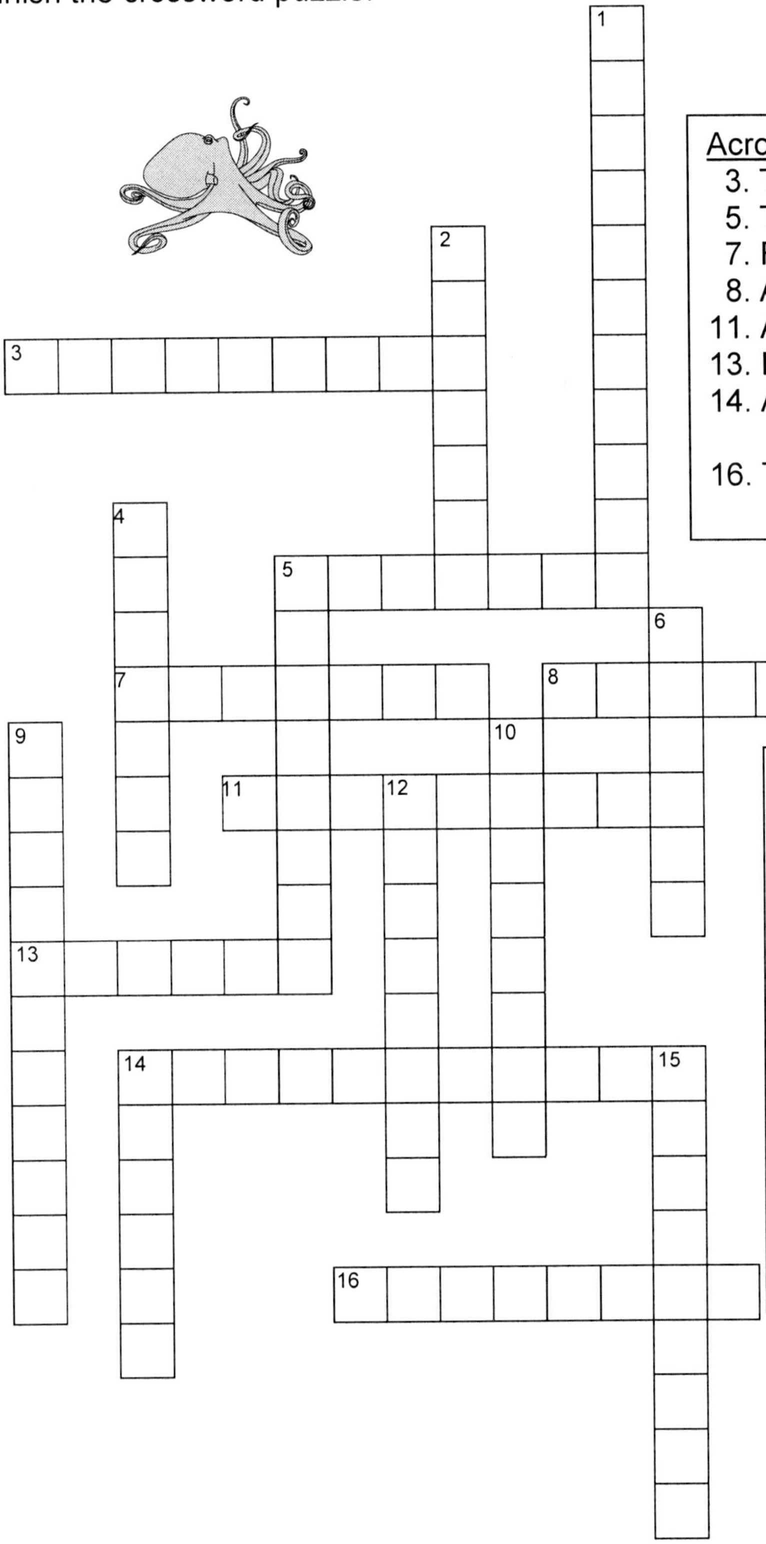

Across:
3. To issue written orders for.
5. To say with authority.
7. Figure with eight angles.
8. A hand-written document.
11. Aware of oneself.
13. Do something with hands.
14. A phrase placed in a sentence to explain.
16. To share feelings of another.

Down:
1. To make by hand.
2. To tell about something before it happens.
4. Eight legged marine animal.
5. An oblique line.
6. Singing together.
9. Measures temperature.
10. Distance across a circle.
12. A measured balance among the parts of something.
14. Letters attached to the front of a word.
15. To put together separate elements to form a whole.

Level 7, Lesson 5 – Words with Greek and Latin prefixes and suffixes

Date: _____

parenthesis	manuscript	sympathy	diagonal
symmetry	diameter	conscious	octagon
synthesis	thermometer	prefix	prescribe
manufacture	predict	octopus	dictate
	manual	unison	

A. Read each clue. Write the list word in the blanks that answers each clue. Read down the shaded cells to find the answer to the question asked. Write the answer to the question in the spaces provided.

1. To issue written orders.
2. Put together separate elements to make a whole.
3. Aware of oneself and one's surroundings.
4. Eight sided figure.
5. To do something with hands.
6. To tell about something before it happens.
7. To say with authority.
8. Letters attached to the beginning of a word.
9. Eight-legged marine animal.

"Shelly was very excited about getting a new camera for her birthday. She could just _____."

Answer: ____ ____ ____ ____ ____ ____ ____   ____ ____ .

B. Copy the following sentence.

Kevin drew a diagonal line through the front page of the manuscript because he did not like the story about the missing thermometer.

_____

_____

_____

_____

Level 7, Lesson 5 – Words with Greek and Latin prefixes and suffixes

Date: _____

Lesson 5
Day 4

parenthesis	manuscript	sympathy	diagonal
symmetry	diameter	conscious	octagon
synthesis	thermometer	prefix	prescribe
manufacture	predict	octopus	dictate
	manual	unison	

A. Write the Latin and Greek origins from Day 1 that are related to each list word. There might be more than one for each list word. The first one has been done for you.

1. manual   manu
2. sympathy _____
3. unison _____
4. dictate _____
5. manufacture _____
6. symmetry _____
7. diameter _____
8. predict _____
9. thermometer _____
10. parenthesis _____
11. octopus _____
12. manuscript _____
13. conscious _____
14. prefix _____
15. diagonal _____
16. octagon _____
17. synthesis _____
18. prescribe _____

B. Write the definition from Day 1 for the list word **parenthesis**.

_____
_____
_____
_____

Level 7, Lesson 5 – Words with Greek and Latin prefixes and suffixes

Lesson 5 - Day 5, Final Test   Correction Area: Date: _____

1. _____   _____
2. _____   _____
3. _____   _____
4. _____   _____
5. _____   _____
6. _____   _____
7. _____   _____
8. _____   _____
9. _____   _____
10. _____   _____
11. _____   _____
12. _____   _____
13. _____   _____
14. _____   _____
15. _____   _____
16. _____   _____
17. _____   _____
18. _____   _____

Carry-over Words: Correction Area:

1. _____   _____
2. _____   _____
3. _____   _____
4. _____   _____

Level 7, Lesson 5 – Words with Greek and Latin prefixes and suffixes

Lesson 6 Review Day 1

Review of words with **cher** and **zher** sounds

List Words

pasture	pleasure	closure	mixture
temperature	feature	disclosure	culture
structure	literature	composure	fracture
measure	creature	furniture	leisure
	treasure	capture	

A. Write the list word that matches each brief definition.

1. Extent or amount.

2. The act of bringing to an end.

3. Making something known.

4. A grassy land.

5. A feeling of enjoyment.

6. To blend two or more ingredients.

7. Something that is built or constructed.

8. Movable items within a house.

9. To take and hold by force.

10. The measurement of heat.

11. To appear calm.

12. A break of something.

13. The main attraction.

14. Written material such as poetry, novels, or essays.

15. Money or jewels of great wealth.

16. A living being.

17. Time of rest or freedom.

18. Traits related to a civilization.

Level 7, Lesson 6, Review of lessons 1-5

Date: _____

Lesson 6 Review Day 2

Review of words with vowel and consonant digraphs

List Words

keyboard	screenplay	shout	prolong
aftershock	airboat	whirlpool	bookkeeper
bargain	chainsaw	feedback	whack
playbook	although	guesthouse	anguish
	author	quench	

A. Find and circle each list word in the puzzle below.

```
W D Q U S J Y U O V P G K N J W
H J Q H R K A K R F R C O I K H
Y F O Z G F L R H R O H O A E I
Y U I J E N P W W H L D B G Y R
T K J F G Z N N S H O W Y R B L
K C A H W U E R B M N F A A O P
B O O K K E E P E R G C L B A O
Q E E K Y T R S W V H H P I R O
U T Z V F K C H T A X Y R Z D L
E F O A Y C S L I H U B F A A K
N P E A O O W N M U O T J F L R
C A N G U I S H B A J U H E W T
H B R P C A M R T F N M S O B S
D T V V W A L T H O U G H E R N
K C A B D E E F E G N A R R A I
```

Level 7, Lesson 6, Review of lessons 1-5

Lesson 6 Review Day 3

Review of words with double consonants

List Words

beginning	fortress	illegible	forgotten
anniversary	stepladder	hallucinate	spaghetti
announcement	suddenly	suppress	correction
accessory	downtrodden	peppermint	embarrass
	allegation	opportunity	

A. Underline the list words in the following sentences.

1. They were beginning their piano lessons.
2. My boss made an allegation that she thought I left work too early on Friday.
3. Cassie did not want to embarrass Vance by giving him a birthday cake at school.
4. Stephen had forgotten to take his medicine.
5. Larry bought a new accessory for his remote control car.
6. The mayor made an announcement that the pool will be closed tomorrow!
7. Brenda had a great opportunity to become the leader of the debate team.
8. Sucking on the peppermint stick eventually made Eric sick.
9. Spaghetti is Kristin's favorite type of pasta.
10. The newspaper made a correction to a story they printed yesterday.
11. The earth shook suddenly as the truck dumped its load of rock on the ground.
12. September is the month of their wedding anniversary.
13. The downtrodden man won a million dollars and was finally set for life.
14. The soldiers gathered in the fortress for protection from the advancing storm.
15. Joy used the stepladder to reach the flour to make bread.
16. Danny's handwriting was completely illegible.
17. As grandpa got older, he would hallucinate if he did not take his medicine.
18. The trial lawyer tried to suppress the admission of guilt by his client.

B. Correctly write the above list words in the order they were found.

1. _____ 2. _____
3. _____ 4. _____
5. _____ 6. _____
7. _____ 8. _____
9. _____ 10. _____
11. _____ 12. _____
13. _____ 14. _____
15. _____ 16. _____
17. _____ 18. _____

Level 7, Lesson 6, Review of lessons 1-5

Date: _____

Lesson 6 Review Day 4

Review of adding er and est to words that end in y

List Words

employer	buyer	scariest	easiest
destroyer	healthier	tiniest	friendliest
sprayer	handier	laziest	loveliest
annoyer	greedier	busiest	craziest
	carrier	sleepiest	

A. Read each clue. Write the list word in the blanks that answers the given clue. Read down the shaded cells to find the answer to the question asked. Write the answer to the question in the space provided.

1. One who does away with.
2. Something that carries something.
3. One who irritates.
4. To be more skilled.
5. Most mentally unstable.
6. The smallest.
7. More of an excessive desire for something.
8. Scatters droplets of liquid.

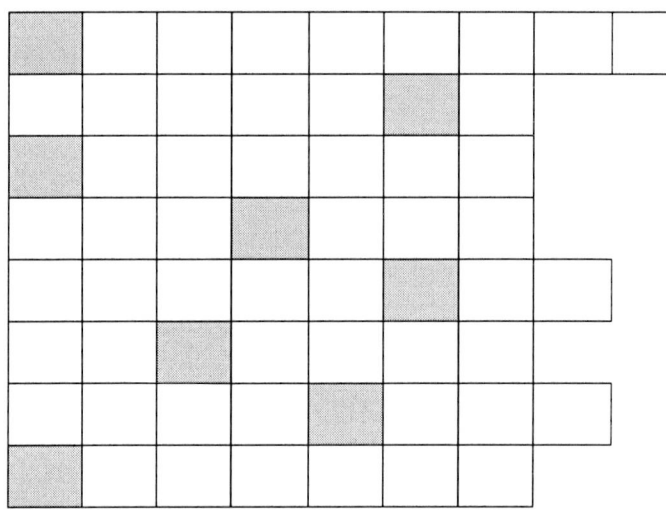

"Rodney desperately wanted to get a job at the Department of Roadways, but he kept running into _____ at every turn."

Answer: ____ ____ ____ ____   ____ ____ ____ ____.

B. Copy the following sentence. **The employer thought the busiest buyer was the friendliest person he had met.**

_____

_____

_____

_____

Level 7, Lesson 6, Review of lessons 1-5

Lesson 6 Review Day 5

Review of words with **Greek** and **Latin prefixes** and **suffixes**

List Words

parenthesis	manuscript	sympathy	diagonal
symmetry	diameter	conscious	octagon
synthesis	thermometer	prefix	prescribe
manufacture	predict	octopus	dictate
	manual	unison	

A. Unscramble the following list words.

naumla

1. _____

ccosnious

2. _____

gooctan

3. _____

tmehromerte

4. _____

diemater

5. _____

maufnacutre

6. _____

usonin

7. _____

dtitcae

8. _____

perrescib

9. _____

ospoctu

10. _____

stsyhneis

11. _____

rpeicdt

12. _____

apsnreethsi

13. _____

mnspraucit

14. _____

aspymthy

15. _____

gdiaanol

16. _____

rpexfi

17. _____

mysterym

18. _____

Level 7, Lesson 6, Review of lessons 1-5

<<Intentionally left blank>>

Words with cian, tion, and sion

1. **Review Your Word List**
Look at the word list below and read each word to yourself. Then review each definition.

The suffix **cian**, when added to a word, means **one who is skilled in**.

The suffix **tion** means **the act of**.

The suffix **sion** means **the act of**.

All of these **suffixes** make a **shun** sound.

List Words/Definitions

Word	Definition
beautician *beautician*	One who is skilled in beauty care.
physician *physician*	One who is skilled in the area of illness and its causes and cures.
politician *politician*	One who is skilled in political endeavors.
dietician *dietician*	One who is skilled in food and nutrition.
optician *optician*	One who is skilled in making lenses and eyeglasses.
mortician *mortician*	One who is skilled in preparing the deceased for burial.
magician *magician*	One who is skilled in performing magic tricks.
pediatrician *pediatrician*	A physician who is skilled in caring for children.
technician *technician*	Someone who is skilled in the industrial arts areas.
attention *attention*	The act of being aware of what is happening around you.
collection *collection*	The act of gathering items together.
celebration *celebration*	The act of celebrating. A party or festival.
satisfaction *satisfaction*	The act of being content or made whole.
confession *confession*	The act of making a statement that admits wrong doing.
operation *operation*	The act of operating. Another name for a surgery.
connection *connection*	The act of connecting. Something that attaches to something else.
introduction *introduction*	The act of introducing. The start or beginning of a book.
imitation *imitation*	The act of imitating. Something that mimics something else.

2. **Take Your Pretest**
Turn to the next page to the Pretest section and your teacher will ask you to write each list word one at a time.

Date: _____

Pretest - Lesson 7: **Correction Area:**

1. _____   _____
2. _____   _____
3. _____   _____
4. _____   _____
5. _____   _____
6. _____   _____
7. _____   _____
8. _____   _____
9. _____   _____
10. _____   _____
11. _____   _____
12. _____   _____
13. _____   _____
14. _____   _____
15. _____   _____
16. _____   _____
17. _____   _____
18. _____   _____

Carry-over Words: **Correction Area:**

1. _____   _____
2. _____   _____
3. _____   _____
4. _____   _____

Level 7, Lesson 7 – Words with **cian**, **tion**, and **sion**

Date: _____

Lesson 7 Day 2

beautician	optician	attention	operation
physician	mortician	collection	connection
politician	magician	celebration	introduction
dietician	pediatrician	satisfaction	imitation
	technician	confession	

A. Read each clue. Write the list word in the blanks that answers each clue. **Unscramble** the highlighted rows to find the answer to the question asked. Write the answer to the question in the spaces provided.

1. One skilled in the area of illness.
2. One skilled in industrial arts.
3. One skilled in making eyeglasses.
4. The act of being content.
5. The act of mimicking another.
6. The act of attaching to something else.
7. The act of gathering items.
8. A statement of wrong doing.
9. One who is skilled in nutrition.

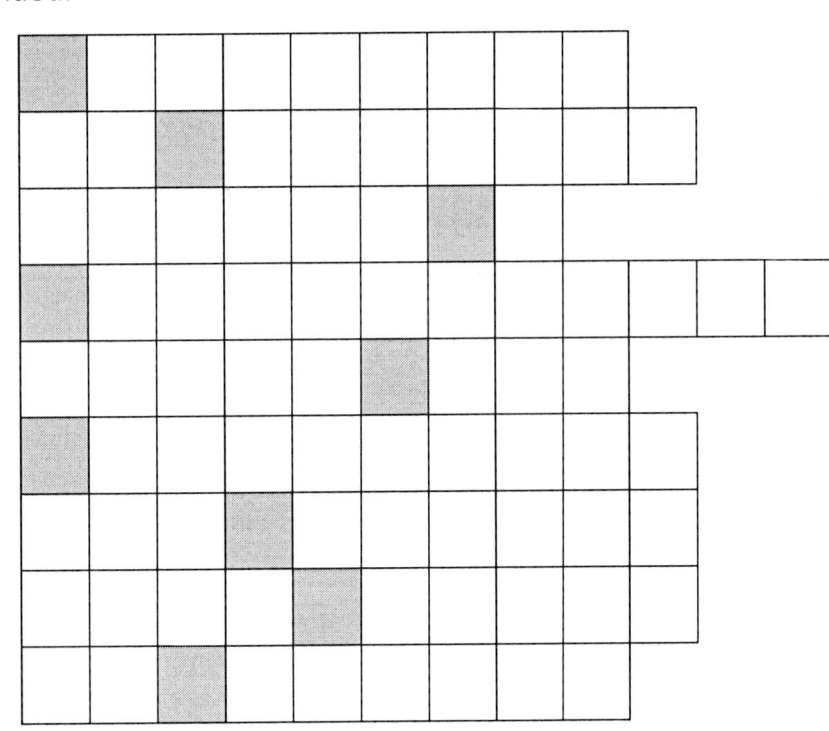

(Unscramble the letters above to find the answer.)

"Did you hear the one about the optician who fell into her lens making solution and made a _____ out of herself?"

Answer: ___ ___ ___ ___ ___ ___ ___ ___

B. Write a list word that matches each clue.

1. One skilled in beauty care.

   _____

2. A surgery.

   _____

3. The act of being aware.

   _____

4. One skilled in preparing another for burial.

   _____

5. One skilled in performing magic tricks.

   _____

6. A party.

   _____

7. The beginning of a book.

   _____

8. A physician skilled in caring for children.

   _____

Level 7, Lesson 7 – Words with **cian**, **tion**, and **sion**

Date: _____

beautician	optician	attention	operation
physician	mortician	collection	connection
politician	magician	celebration	introduction
dietician	pediatrician	satisfaction	imitation
	technician	confession	

A. Write the list words that complete each sentence.

1. The _____ fixed the car.
2. The robber told the police his _____.
3. The counterfeit purse was an _____ of the real thing.
4. Her favorite book had an interesting _____.
5. The _____ fixed Marcia's hair perfectly.
6. The _____ made my glasses very quickly.
7. Lauren gave her undivided _____ to the teacher.
8. Grandpa had quite a _____ of stamps.
9. Riding his bike in the breeze gave Tim much _____.
10. Dad's _____ told him he had a nasal infection.
11. The _____ prepared the remains for burial.
12. The _____ prepared a nutritious menu for our family.
13. The _____ gave a speech as she campaigned to be mayor.
14. Amy had to have an _____ on her broken foot.
15. Todd used a piece of wire to make an electrical _____.
16. The _____ made his assistant disappear.
17. They held quite a _____ for grandma's 100th birthday.
18. Sally took her sick baby to see the _____.

B. Write the definition from Day 1 for the list word **technician**.

_____
_____
_____
_____

Level 7, Lesson 7 – Words with **cian**, **tion**, and **sion**   40

Lesson 7 Day 4

beautician	optician	attention	operation
physician	mortician	collection	connection
politician	magician	celebration	introduction
dietician	pediatrician	satisfaction	imitation
	technician	confession	

A. Draw a line to connect each list word with its definition.

Word	Definition
celebration	Something that attaches to something else.
satisfaction	The start of a book.
confession	Someone who is skilled in industrial arts areas.
connection	One skilled in making eyeglasses.
mortician	A physician who specializes in caring for children.
optician	A statement that admits wrong doing.
introduction	Another name for a surgery.
operation	One who does magic tricks.
magician	One who has skill in preparing the deceased for burial.
pediatrician	The act of being content or made whole.
collection	One who is skilled in food and nutrition.
attention	A party or festival.
dietician	One who is skilled in political endeavors.
politician	One who is skilled in the area of illness.
physician	Being aware of what is happening around you.
beautician	The act of gathering items together.
imitation	Something that mimics something else.
technician	One who is skilled in beauty care.

B. Copy the following sentence. **After Joe's confession, the sheriff and his staff had a celebration with an imitation cake.**

_____

_____

_____

Level 7, Lesson 7 – Words with **cian**, **tion**, and **sion**

Date: _____

Lesson 7 - Day 5, Final Test

Correction Area:

1. _____ _____
2. _____ _____
3. _____ _____
4. _____ _____
5. _____ _____
6. _____ _____
7. _____ _____
8. _____ _____
9. _____ _____
10. _____ _____
11. _____ _____
12. _____ _____
13. _____ _____
14. _____ _____
15. _____ _____
16. _____ _____
17. _____ _____
18. _____ _____

Carry-over Words:

Correction Area:

1. _____ _____
2. _____ _____
3. _____ _____
4. _____ _____

Level 7, Lesson 7 – Words with **cian**, **tion**, and **sion**

Lesson 8 Day 1

Date: _____

Words with **able**, **ible**, and **ous**

1. **Review Your Word List**
   Look at the word list below and read each word to yourself. Then review each definition.

   - The suffix **ous** means **full of** or **having the characteristic of**.
   - The suffixes **able** and **ible** mean **able to**, **worthy of**, or **tending to**.

   The following rules can often help you decide if a word should end in **able** or **ible**.

   - If you remove **able** from a word, you are left with a complete word.
     retractable - **able** = **retract**
     The final **e** is usually dropped when adding **able**. **value** + **able** = **valuable**

   - If you remove **ible** from a word, you are usually not left with a complete word.
     compatible - **ible** = **compat** (not a word)
     There are some exceptions to this rule. **convertible** - **ible** = **convert** (a word)

   If you are not sure about a word, you should consult a **dictionary**.

List Words/Definitions

adventurous *adventurous*		**negligible** *negligible*	
• Full of adventure. Ready to take on new challenges or danger.		• Worthy of neglect due to little value or consequence.	
continuous *continuous*		**audible** *audible*	
• Having the characteristic of not ending.		• Able to be heard.	
delirious *delirious*		**convertible** *convertible*	
• Having the characteristic of delirium. A condition of having a confused mind.		• Able to be converted. An automobile that has a soft, removable top.	
frivolous *frivolous*		**valuable** *valuable*	
• Full of frivolity. Something that lacks serious intent.		• Worthy of value. Something having great worth.	
hazardous *hazardous*		**sizeable** *sizable*	
• Full of hazard. Dangerous and high risk.		• Tending to be large. Something that has considerable size.	
infamous *infamous*		**retractable** *retractable*	
• Having the characteristic of an evil reputation.		• Something able to be pulled back.	
responsible *responsible*		**negotiable** *negotiable*	
• Able to be trusted or depended upon.		• Able to be negotiated. A flexible exchange for settlement.	
permissible *permissible*		**measurable** *measurable*	
• Able to be allowed.		• Something able to be measured.	
compatible *compatible*		**desirable** *desirable*	
• Able to be agreeable with others.		• Something worthy of desire. Wanted.	

2. **Take Your Pretest**
   Turn to the next page to the Pretest section and your teacher will ask you to write each list word one at a time.

Level 7, Lesson 8 – Words with **able**, **ible**, and **ous**

Date: _____

Pretest - Lesson 8:
Correction Area:

1. _____
2. _____
3. _____
4. _____
5. _____
6. _____
7. _____
8. _____
9. _____
10. _____
11. _____
12. _____
13. _____
14. _____
15. _____
16. _____
17. _____
18. _____

Carry-over Words:
Correction Area:

1. _____
2. _____
3. _____
4. _____

Level 7, Lesson 8 – Words with **able**, **ible**, and **ous**

Date: _____

Lesson 8 Day 2

adventurous	hazardous	negligible	retractable
continuous	infamous	audible	negotiable
delirious	responsible	convertible	measurable
frivolous	permissible	valuable	desirable
	compatible	sizeable	

A. Find and circle each list word in the puzzle below.

```
H  A  Z  A  R  D  O  U  S  W  D  B  E  E  C
S  U  O  R  U  T  N  E  V  D  A  Y  L  F  O
E  F  D  U  E  G  W  A  X  N  S  B  B  R  N
S  L  G  E  V  A  L  P  E  U  I  E  I  I  T
U  D  B  X  L  U  F  G  H  T  Z  L  T  V  I
O  N  S  A  A  I  O  D  R  M  E  B  A  O  N
M  Z  E  B  T  T  R  E  T  Y  A  I  P  L  U
A  T  L  G  I  C  V  I  S  K  B  S  M  O  O
F  E  A  A  L  N  A  N  O  N  L  N  O  U  U
N  O  B  A  O  I  W  R  Z  U  E  O  C  S  S
I  L  F  C  I  I  G  S  T  G  S  P  O  Y  K
E  Z  E  L  B  A  R  I  S  E  D  S  G  R  F
T  E  L  B  I  D  U  A  B  P  R  E  X  X  W
P  E  R  M  I  S  S  I  B  L  E  R  A  M  Q
E  L  B  A  R  U  S  A  E  M  E  H  A  D  D
```

B. Write the definition from Day 1 for the list word **convertible**.

_____

_____

_____

_____

Level 7, Lesson 8 – Words with **able**, **ible**, and **ous**

Lesson 8 Day 3

adventurous	hazardous	negligible	retractable
continuous	infamous	audible	negotiable
delirious	responsible	convertible	measurable
frivolous	permissible	valuable	desirable
	compatible	sizeable	

Date: _____

A. Unscramble the following list words.

    cmaioptble

1. _____

    szeialbe

2. _____

    ofrilovus

3. _____

    dseairble

4. _____

    vadteunrous

5. _____

    hzaaordus

6. _____

    nigileeglb

7. _____

    esmaurable

8. _____

    neiotgable

9. _____

    duleiiros

10. _____

    prensosible

11. _____

    diauble

12. _____

    rtetracable

13. _____

    tcoinnuous

14. _____

    fainmous

15. _____

    pmserisible

16. _____

    vconeirtble

17. _____

    lvabuale

18. _____

B. Copy the following sentence. **I once owned a convertible in high school that is now very desirable and valuable.**

_____

_____

_____

_____

Level 7, Lesson 8 – Words with **able**, **ible**, and **ous**

Lesson 8 Day 4

adventurous	hazardous	negligible	retractable
continuous	infamous	audible	negotiable
delirious	responsible	convertible	measurable
frivolous	permissible	valuable	desirable
	compatible	sizeable	

A. Read the following sentences and write on the lines below the list words you see.

The adventurous and infamous men had become delirious after making a frivolous decision to drink water from a continuous but hazardous stream. They were searching for a desirable, valuable, and measurable treasure that was sizeable.

1. _____ 2. _____
3. _____ 4. _____
5. _____ 6. _____
7. _____ 8. _____
9. _____ 10. _____

The car for sale that had a retractable roof was compatible and permissible with the convertible. When the roof was up, there was negligible audible wind noise. The responsible party for its sale said the price was negotiable.

11. _____ 12. _____
13. _____ 14. _____
15. _____ 16. _____
17. _____ 18. _____

B. Finish each list word. Use each list word only once.

1. h_____ 2. ____tr_____
3. ____z_____ 4. ____sir_____
5. ____mp_____ 6. ____go_____
7. ____iv_____ 8. _____gi_____
9. v_____ 10. _____rt_____
11. ____li_____ 12. ____ea_____
13. p_____ 14. ____sp_____
15. ____ud_____ 16. _____tin_____
17. in_____ 18. ____ve_____

Level 7, Lesson 8 – Words with **able**, **ible**, and **ous**

47

Lesson 8 - Day 5, Final Test

Date: _____

Correction Area:

1. _____
2. _____
3. _____
4. _____
5. _____
6. _____
7. _____
8. _____
9. _____
10. _____
11. _____
12. _____
13. _____
14. _____
15. _____
16. _____
17. _____
18. _____

Carry-over Words:

Correction Area:

1. _____
2. _____
3. _____
4. _____

Level 7, Lesson 8 – Words with **able**, **ible**, and **ous**

Date: _____

Words with **under**

1. **Review Your Word List**
   Look at the word list below and read each word to yourself. Then review each definition.

List Words/Definitions

blunder *blunder*	undergrowth *undergrowth*
• A silly mistake.	• The plants growing beneath taller trees in a forest.
founder *founder*	underachieve *underachieve*
• One who establishes something.	• To achieve less than was expected.
grounder *grounder*	underrated *underrated*
• A hit baseball that travels along the ground.	• To be undervalued.
flounder *flounder*	underarm *underarm*
• To move in a clumsy way. To behave awkwardly.	• The lower part of the arm where it meets the torso. Armpit.
asunder *asunder*	undercover *undercover*
• To be in separate parts or pieces.	• Doing something in secret.
launder *launder*	underdog *underdog*
• To wash or clean clothing.	• Someone who is not favored to win or succeed.
misunderstand *misunderstand*	underestimate *underestimate*
• To understand incorrectly.	• To make too low of an estimate.
plunder *plunder*	undergraduate *undergraduate*
• To rob or steal by force.	• A person attending the first four years of college.
thunder *thunder*	underground *underground*
• A loud boom that usually occurs after a lightning strike.	• A place under the surface of the earth.

2. **Take Your Pretest**
   Turn to the next page to the Pretest section and your teacher will ask you to write each list word one at a time.

Level 7, Lesson 9 – Words with **under**

Date: _____

Pretest - Lesson 9:   **Correction Area:**

1. _____   _____
2. _____   _____
3. _____   _____
4. _____   _____
5. _____   _____
6. _____   _____
7. _____   _____
8. _____   _____
9. _____   _____
10. _____   _____
11. _____   _____
12. _____   _____
13. _____   _____
14. _____   _____
15. _____   _____
16. _____   _____
17. _____   _____
18. _____   _____

Carry-over Words: **Correction Area:**

1. _____   _____
2. _____   _____
3. _____   _____
4. _____   _____

Level 7, Lesson 9 – Words with **under**

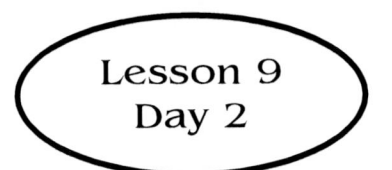

Date: _____

blunder	asunder	undergrowth	underdog
founder	launder	underachieve	underestimate
grounder	misunderstand	underrated	undergraduate
flounder	plunder	underarm	underground
	thunder	undercover	

A. Write each group of three list words in alphabetical order.

underarm, underachieve, underestimate

1. _____ 2. _____ 3. _____

underground, undergraduate, undercover

4. _____ 5. _____ 6. _____

underdog, underrated, underarm

7. _____ 8. _____ 9. _____

founder, flounder, launder

10. _____ 11. _____ 12. _____

misunderstand, undergrowth, plunder

13. _____ 14. _____ 15. _____

grounder, blunder, asunder

16. _____ 17. _____ 18. _____

flounder, thunder, founder

19. _____ 20. _____ 21. _____

underarm, undergraduate, underachieve

22. _____ 23. _____ 24. _____

misunderstand, asunder, grounder

25. _____ 26. _____ 27. _____

underground, undergrowth, undergraduate

28. _____ 29. _____ 30. _____

Level 7, Lesson 9 – Words with **under**

Lesson 9
Day 3

Date: _____

blunder	asunder	undergrowth	underdog
founder	launder	underachieve	underestimate
grounder	misunderstand	underrated	undergraduate
flounder	plunder	underarm	underground
	thunder	undercover	

A. Finish the crossword puzzle.

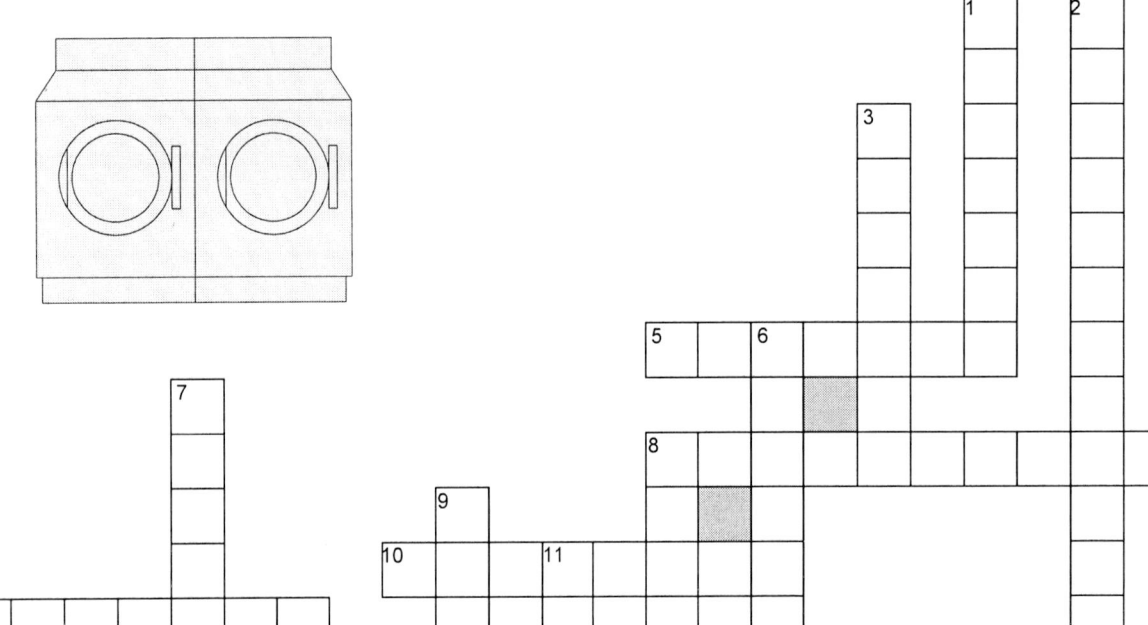

Down:
1. To be in separate parts.
2. To make too low of an estimate.
3. A silly mistake.
6. Under the earth's crust.
7. Loud boom that follows lightning.
8. Where the arm meets the torso.
9. To rob by force.
11. First years of college.
12. A baseball that travels along the ground.
14. Not favored to win.
16. To understand incorrectly.

Across:
4. To clean clothing.
5. One who establishes something.
8. Achieve less than expected.
10. To move in a clumsy way.
13. To be undervalued.
14. To do in secret.
15. Plants growing beneath taller trees.

Level 7, Lesson 9 – Words with **under**

Lesson 9 Day 4

Date: _____

blunder	asunder	undergrowth	underdog
founder	launder	underachieve	underestimate
grounder	misunderstand	underrated	undergraduate
flounder	plunder	underarm	underground
	thunder	undercover	

A. Write the definition from Day 1 for the list word **undergraduate**.

_____

_____

_____

_____

B. Write a short paragraph below using at least four list words.

_____

_____

_____

_____

_____

C. Underline the misspelled list words in the following sentences. Write the misspelled words correctly on the lines provided.

1. The undercuver spy who lived undergrownd was underrayted as a huge undurdogg.

   _____   _____

   _____   _____

2. Although they would flownder and underestuhmate the size of the treasure, they would nevertheless plundur and tear it asunder.

   _____   _____

   _____   _____

3. The undergraduwate could underacheeve on his final exam.

   _____   _____

Level 7, Lesson 9 – Words with **under**

Lesson 9- Day 5, Final Test

Date: _____

Correction Area:

1. _____ _____
2. _____ _____
3. _____ _____
4. _____ _____
5. _____ _____
6. _____ _____
7. _____ _____
8. _____ _____
9. _____ _____
10. _____ _____
11. _____ _____
12. _____ _____
13. _____ _____
14. _____ _____
15. _____ _____
16. _____ _____
17. _____ _____
18. _____ _____

Carry-over Words:

Correction Area:

1. _____ _____
2. _____ _____
3. _____ _____
4. _____ _____

Level 7, Lesson 9 – Words with **under**

Date: _____

Words with the **schwa** sound

1. **Review Your Word List**
   Look at the word list below and read each word to yourself. Then review each definition.

   The **schwa** sound is the **uh** sound made by one or more vowels. The vowels in a word that make the **schwa** sound do not make the usual long or short vowel sounds, but these vowels make the **uh** sound. For example, the vowel **o** in the word **seldom** makes a **schwa** (**uh**) sound. The vowels **ou** in the word **curious** make the **schwa** (**uh**) sound. When writing pronunciations of words with schwa sounds (usually used in dictionaries), an upside-down **ə** is used to represent the **schwa** sound. Example: d<u>o</u>z<u>e</u>n = dəz-ən

   The **schwa** sound is underlined in the list words below. Some of the words have two **schwa** sounds.

   ### List Words/Definitions

Word		Word	
tr<u>u</u>sted — Worthy of reliance or confidence.	*trusted*	ple<u>a</u>sant — Nice or inviting.	*pleasant*
d<u>o</u>zen — Twelve of something.	*dozen*	seld<u>o</u>m — Not very often.	*seldom*
tak<u>e</u>n — Something that is snatched or removed.	*taken*	<u>o</u>ther — Different from the one or ones already mentioned or implied.	*other*
pres<u>i</u>d<u>e</u>nt — One who is in charge of a company or country.	*president*	hist<u>o</u>ry — Events that happened in the past.	*history*
mount<u>ai</u>n — A tall geographic land mass.	*mountain*	<u>a</u>gain — To repeat or do over.	*again*
fam<u>ou</u>s — Known by many.	*famous*	en<u>e</u>my — One who opposes or is at war with another.	*enemy*
stenc<u>i</u>l — A guide to assist in writing or painting.	*stencil*	est<u>i</u>mate — To make a guess at something.	*estimate*
c<u>o</u>nfr<u>o</u>nt — Rise to face a challenge.	*confront*	<u>a</u>dj<u>u</u>st — To slightly modify something to make it correct.	*adjust*
probl<u>e</u>m — A situation that has to be resolved.	*problem*	curi<u>ou</u>s — Eager or interested to learn.	*curious*

2. **Take Your Pretest**
   Turn to the next page to the Pretest section and your teacher will ask you to write each list word one at a time.

Level 7, Lesson 10 – Words with the **schwa** sound

Date: _____

Pretest - Lesson 10:   Correction Area:

1. _____   _____
2. _____   _____
3. _____   _____
4. _____   _____
5. _____   _____
6. _____   _____
7. _____   _____
8. _____   _____
9. _____   _____
10. _____   _____
11. _____   _____
12. _____   _____
13. _____   _____
14. _____   _____
15. _____   _____
16. _____   _____
17. _____   _____
18. _____   _____

Carry-over Words: Correction Area:

1. _____   _____
2. _____   _____
3. _____   _____
4. _____   _____

Level 7, Lesson 10 – Words with the **schwa** sound

Date: _____

Lesson 10
Day 2

trusted	mountain	pleasant	enemy
dozen	famous	seldom	estimate
taken	stencil	other	adjust
president	confront	history	curious
	problem	again	

A. Use the following code to finish the sentences.

A	B	C	D	E	F	G	H	I	J	K	L	M	N	O	P	Q	R	S	T	U	V	W	X	Y	Z
Ω	☺	⊡	❋	👍	☻	❄	✿	✎	📬	◇	◆	❀	⌘	❖	✈	●	⊙	⏲	★	✚	×	⧖	⌒	☎	📖

1. We all __ __ __ __ __ __ __ Allen with our money.
   ★ ⊙ ✚ ⏲ ★ 👍 ❋

2. Breaking the lamp was going to be a serious __ __ __ __ __ __ __.
   ✈ ⊙ ❖ ☺ ◆ 👍 ❀

3. Shelli wanted to ride the coaster __ __ __ __ __.
   Ω ❋ Ω ✎ ⌘

4. The bear was __ __ __ __ __ __ __ as to what was in the jar.
   ⊡ ✚ ⊙ ✎ ❖ ✚ ⏲

5. The scientist had to slightly __ __ __ __ __ __ his formula.
   Ω ❋ ⊡ ✚ ⏲ ★

6. Their __ __ __ __ __ was approaching fast.
   👍 ⌘ 👍 ❀ ☎

7. Debbie used a __ __ __ __ __ __ __ to paint the mural.
   ⏲ ★ 👍 ⌘ ⊡ ✎ ◆

8. Darlene became __ __ __ __ __ __ after winning the race.
   ☻ Ω ❋ ❖ ✚ ⏲

9. The __ __ __ __ __ __ __ __ __ stood to address the group.
   ✈ ⊙ 👍 ⏲ ✎ ❋ 👍 ⌘ ★

10. Sherri was very __ __ __ __ __ __ __ __ after waking from her nap.
    ✈ ◆ 👍 Ω ⏲ Ω ⌘ ★

11. With our long rope, we were ready to attack the __ __ __ __ __ __ __ __.
    ❀ ❖ ✚ ⌘ ★ Ω ✎ ❀

12. This seat is __ __ __ __ __.
    ★ Ω ◇ 👍 ⌘

13. You should have taken the __ __ __ __ __ road because we are now lost.
    ❖ ★ ✿ 👍 ⊙

14. The __ __ __ __ __ donuts look delicious.
    ❋ ❖ 📖 👍 ⌘

15. Andrew __ __ __ __ __ __ ate his salad.
    ⏲ 👍 ◆ ❋ ❖ ❀

16. I __ __ __ __ __ __ __ __ that we will receive two inches of rain.
    👍 ⏲ ★ ✎ ❋ Ω ★ 👍

17. Emily was ready to __ __ __ __ __ __ __ __ her fear of heights.
    ⊡ ❖ ⌘ ☺ ⊙ ❖ ⌘ ★

18. __ __ __ __ __ __ __ was Emma's favorite subject.
    ✿ ✎ ⏲ ★ ❖ ⊙ ☎

Level 7, Lesson 10 – Words with the **schwa** sound

Lesson 10
Day 3

Date: _____

trusted	mountain	pleasant	enemy
dozen	famous	seldom	estimate
taken	stencil	other	adjust
president	confront	history	curious
	problem	again	

A. Write the list words that match these dictionary pronunciations.

pre-zə-dənt

1. _____

ple-zənt

2. _____

e-nə-mē

3. _____

es-tə-māt

4. _____

trəst-ed

5. _____

maún-tən

6. _____

prŏ-bləm

7. _____

sel-dəm

8. _____

ə-ther

9. _____

his-tə-rē

10. _____

kən-'frənt

11. _____

sten-səl

12. _____

də-zən

13. _____

tāk-ən

14. _____

fā-məs

15. _____

ə-gen

16. _____

kyúr-ē-əs

17. _____

ə-jəst

18. _____

Level 7, Lesson 10 – Words with the **schwa** sound

Date: _____

Lesson 10 Day 4

trusted	mountain	pleasant	enemy
dozen	famous	seldom	estimate
taken	stencil	other	adjust
president	confront	history	curious
	problem	again	

A. Underline the word in parentheses that makes sense to complete the sentence.

1. Jason had a (confront, problem) with his math assignment.
2. The (president, dozen) of our company stopped by to greet the workers.
3. The monkey was (adjust, curious) about his surroundings.
4. You need to (seldom, estimate) how much this bill will be.
5. Brad was a serious tennis player and treated me like an (enemy, trusted).
6. Christine (confront, trusted) me enough to give me her keys.
7. Ben needed to (again, confront) his enemy in order to work things out.
8. Kristin rode the pony (again, other) because she loved its spots.
9. Judy and Devin took a (adjust, pleasant) ride through the country.
10. Connie had already (taken, other) her science test.
11. Bonnie would (famous, seldom) go to work as her schedule required.
12. Stewart climbed the (mountain, history) made of red stone.
13. Jacob became (history, famous) after starring in the movie.
14. A (estimate, dozen) donuts ended up being the right amount for the group.
15. Cathy used a (mountain, stencil) to paint the letters on the sign.
16. Jamie wanted the (other, problem) bicycle with the blue paint.
17. Western (history, famous) taught us many lessons in mining gold.
18. Kurt needs to (seldom, adjust) his schedule to meet with the president of the bank.

B. Copy the following sentence. **Sharon had a problem when it came time to confront her enemy who lived in the famous mountain.**

_____

_____

_____

Level 7, Lesson 10 – Words with the **schwa** sound

Date: _____

Lesson 10 - Day 5, Final Test <u>Correction Area</u>:

1. _____   _____
2. _____   _____
3. _____   _____
4. _____   _____
5. _____   _____
6. _____   _____
7. _____   _____
8. _____   _____
9. _____   _____
10. _____   _____
11. _____   _____
12. _____   _____
13. _____   _____
14. _____   _____
15. _____   _____
16. _____   _____
17. _____   _____
18. _____   _____

<u>Carry-over Words</u>:   <u>Correction Area</u>:

1. _____   _____
2. _____   _____
3. _____   _____
4. _____   _____

Level 7, Lesson 10 – Words with the **schwa** sound

Date: _____

Words with the f sound using f, ff, ph, and gh

1. **Review Your List Words**
   Look at the list words below and read each word to yourself. Then review each definition.

List Words/Definitions

pharmacy *pharmacy* • A place that dispenses medicine. A drugstore.	**microphone** *microphone* • A device which receives and transmits sound.
rougher *rougher* • To be more course or uneven than something else.	**emphatic** *emphatic* • Spoken with emphasis or excitement.
triumph *triumph* • To win or conquer something.	**autograph** *autograph* • A person's own signature or handwriting.
pheasant *pheasant* • A large, colorful game bird.	**facility** *facility* • An area that provides a particular service.
effective *effective* • Something that is capable of producing an intended result.	**farrier** *farrier* • One who shoes horses.
baffled *baffled* • To be confused.	**fragile** *fragile* • Very delicate and breakable.
suffocate *suffocate* • To deprive of oxygen.	**future** *future* • A time after this moment.
raffle *raffle* • A contest where a random winner is drawn.	**favorite** *favorite* • Desired above all others.
affiliate *affiliate* • One who has a business connection.	**fantastic** *fantastic* • Extraordinarily good.

2. **Take Your Pretest**
   Turn to the next page to the Pretest section and your teacher will ask you to write each list word one at a time.

Level 7, Lesson 11 – Words with the **f** sound using **f, ff, ph,** and **gh**   61

Date: _____

Pretest - Lesson 11:   **Correction Area:**

1. _____   _____
2. _____   _____
3. _____   _____
4. _____   _____
5. _____   _____
6. _____   _____
7. _____   _____
8. _____   _____
9. _____   _____
10. _____   _____
11. _____   _____
12. _____   _____
13. _____   _____
14. _____   _____
15. _____   _____
16. _____   _____
17. _____   _____
18. _____   _____

Carry-over Words: **Correction Area:**

1. _____   _____
2. _____   _____
3. _____   _____
4. _____   _____

Level 7, Lesson 11 – Words with the **f** sound using **f**, **ff**, **ph**, and **gh**

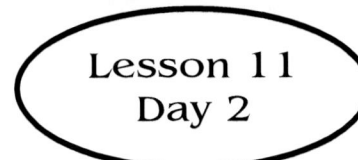

Date: _____

Lesson 11 Day 2

pharmacy	effective	microphone	fragile
rougher	baffled	emphatic	future
triumph	suffocate	autograph	favorite
pheasant	raffle	facility	fantastic
	affiliate	farrier	

A. Fill in each sentence with the correct list word.

1. The _____ put new horseshoes on the thoroughbred.
2. Mom did a _____ job making those cookies; they were delicious!
3. Our basketball team enjoyed its _____ over the visiting team.
4. The sand was _____ on my feet than the smooth sidewalk.
5. The _____ has everything we need to fix the car.
6. I won a television at the charity _____.
7. Bobby was lucky to get the _____ of his favorite singer.
8. The glass lamp was very _____ and had to be handled with care.
9. Sheila is looking forward to her _____ as a doctor.
10. Jerry picked up his medicine at the _____.
11. The long handled brush was _____ in painting the high places.
12. The chocolate candy was his _____ treat.
13. He spoke into the _____ so all could hear him.
14. Ivan was _____ by her confusing answer.
15. Patty felt like she was going to _____ in the hot, closed room.
16. Tricia was _____ in that she did not want to go out to eat.
17. The _____ scared us when it suddenly took flight in front of us.
18. Millie collaborated as an _____ with a company selling candy.

B. Write a short paragraph below using at least four list words.

_____

_____

_____

_____

Level 7, Lesson 11 – Words with the **f** sound using **f, ff, ph,** and **gh**   63

Date: _____

Lesson 11 Day 3

pharmacy	effective	microphone	fragile
rougher	baffled	emphatic	future
triumph	suffocate	autograph	favorite
pheasant	raffle	facility	fantastic
	affiliate	farrier	

A. Find and circle each list word in the puzzle below.

```
F D O I Y E M R K M R K M C E
I Q Q N L T E E I O P Q I A M
E K F F M H I C M G C T Z A P
X T F N G S R L F E S U D H H
P A A U H O Y A I A Q G J I A
R H O C P E V I T C E F F E T
V R A H O O R N G H A O X Q I
Z R O R R F A M W P R F L O C
J N E I M F F T N A S A E H P
E I T I I A X U T R E D L C B
G E A N R S C O S G R N I I X
H P M U I R T Y M O U M G A D
A F F I L I A T E T T F A H Z
B A F F L E D F F U U G R U B
V E U Y V I W G M A F V F G P
```

B. Copy the following sentence. **The man from the facility used the microphone in the pharmacy to announce the winner of the raffle.**

_____

_____

_____

Level 7, Lesson 11 – Words with the **f** sound using **f**, **ff**, **ph**, and **gh**

Lesson 11 Day 4

pharmacy	effective	microphone	fragile
rougher	baffled	emphatic	future
triumph	suffocate	autograph	favorite
pheasant	raffle	facility	fantastic
	affiliate	farrier	

A. Finish each list word. Use each list word only once.

1. _____ar_____y
2. _____rr_____
3. r_____
4. _____ha_____
5. _____tu_____
6. _____gi_____
7. __af_____
8. ___uf_____
9. _____ra_____
10. _____vo_____
11. _____iu_____
12. _____sa_____
13. _____fe_____
14. _____fl_____
15. _____op_____
16. _____ia_____
17. _____ci_____
18. _____st_____

B. Write the definition from Day 1 for the list word **facility**.

_____
_____
_____
_____

C. Write the definition from Day 1 for the list word **emphatic**.

_____
_____
_____
_____

Level 7, Lesson 11 – Words with the **f** sound using **f, ff, ph,** and **gh**

Date: _____

Lesson 11 - Day 5, Final Test

Correction Area:

1. _____
2. _____
3. _____
4. _____
5. _____
6. _____
7. _____
8. _____
9. _____
10. _____
11. _____
12. _____
13. _____
14. _____
15. _____
16. _____
17. _____
18. _____

Carry-over Words:

Correction Area:

1. _____
2. _____
3. _____
4. _____

Level 7, Lesson 11 – Words with the **f** sound using **f**, **ff**, **ph**, and **gh**

Lesson 12 Review Day 1

Review of words with **cian**, **tion**, and **sion**

List Words

beautician	optician	attention	operation
physician	mortician	collection	connection
politician	magician	celebration	introduction
dietician	pediatrician	satisfaction	imitation
	technician	confession	

A. Find and circle each list word in the puzzle below.

```
N N X C N P M A G I C I A N B I
A O T S E O H M P K D F A A E M
I I I G T L I Y B P W I X I A I
C T X T S N E T S F C K L C U T
I C G C N H A B C I B S G I T A
T U N O S E V I R E C H Z T I T
I D Q S V B T T C A N I P P C I
L O S O F M A T D I T N A O I O
O R S A T I S F A C T I O N A N
P T D W D K U F W H W E O C N K
Y N T E C H N I C I A N I N A S
W I P N O I T C E L L O C D I D
N O I S S E F N O C H G S M A J
S R W J G O P E R A T I O N M A
I T D N A I C I T R O M R E W D
```

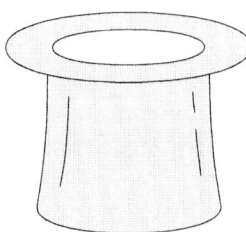

Level 7, Lesson 12, Review of lessons 7-11

Date: _____

Lesson 12 Review Day 2

Review of words with **able**, **ible**, and **ous**

List Words

adventurous	hazardous	negligible	retractable
continuous	infamous	audible	negotiable
delirious	responsible	convertible	measurable
frivolous	permissible	valuable	desirable
	compatible	sizeable	

A. Underline the word in parentheses that makes sense to complete the sentence.

1. The (sizeable, desirable) mass of ice was moving toward the shore.
2. Gold is a very (frivolous, desirable) and precious material.
3. Their progress was (hazardous, measurable) as the building grew taller.
4. The price to be paid for the new car was (audible, negotiable).
5. Wayne was (infamous, delirious) after being awake for three days straight.
6. Maria and Kelly were (adventurous, audible) when looking for fun.
7. The lawsuit was (negligible, frivolous) as it had no chance of succeeding.
8. Henry was (responsible, convertible) for keeping track of our money.
9. El Guapo was (compatible, infamous) for doing bad things.
10. The impact of dropping a pebble into the pool was (retractable, negligible).
11. The hands on the clock made an (hazardous, audible) noise as the clock worked.
12. The new car was a (convertible, permissible) with a soft, black top.
13. The leaky faucet made a (compatible, continuous) dripping noise.
14. It was (valuable, permissible) for Beth to ride her bike in the empty parking lot.
15. Walking close to the active volcano is considered (measurable, hazardous).
16. The awning was (negotiable, retractable) and could be opened and shut.
17. The huge diamond was extremely (valuable, hazardous).
18. The disc drive was not (adventurous, compatible) with his new computer.

B. Write the list words that you underlined above.

1. _____ 2. _____
3. _____ 4. _____
5. _____ 6. _____
7. _____ 8. _____
9. _____ 10. _____
11. _____ 12. _____
13. _____ 14. _____
15. _____ 16. _____
17. _____ 18. _____

Level 7, Lesson 12, Review of lessons 7-11

Lesson 12 Review Day 3

Review of words with **under**

List Words

blunder	asunder	undergrowth	underdog
founder	launder	underachieve	underestimate
grounder	misunderstand	underrated	undergraduate
flounder	plunder	underarm	underground
	thunder	undercover	

A. Write each group of three list words in alphabetical order.

underestimate, underachieve, underarm

1. _____ 2. _____ 3. _____

underrated, underdog, underground

4. _____ 5. _____ 6. _____

undercover, underestimate, undergraduate

7. _____ 8. _____ 9. _____

thunder, launder, blunder

10. _____ 11. _____ 12. _____

grounder, flounder, founder

13. _____ 14. _____ 15. _____

asunder, misunderstand, plunder

16. _____ 17. _____ 18. _____

undergrowth, founder, blunder

19. _____ 20. _____ 21. _____

underestimated, underground, underarm

22. _____ 23. _____ 24. _____

thunder, blunder, founder

25. _____ 26. _____ 27. _____

Level 7, Lesson 12, Review of lessons 7-11

Lesson 12 Review Day 4

Review of words with the schwa sound

Date: _____

List Words

trusted	mountain	pleasant	enemy
dozen	famous	seldom	estimate
taken	stencil	other	adjust
president	confront	history	curious
	problem	again	

A. Finish the crossword puzzle.

Down:
1. Eager or interested.
2. Face a challenge.
4. Snatched or removed.
6. Nice or inviting.
7. Twelve of something.
8. Slightly modify.
11. A guess.
12. Events in the past.
15. One who opposes you.

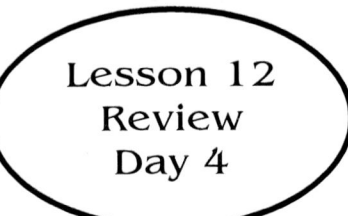

Across:
3. Different from the one already mentioned.
5. Known by many.
6. One who is in charge.
9. To repeat or do over.
10. Not very often.
13. A guide to assist in writing.
14. Worthy of confidence.
16. A tall land mass.
17. A situation to be resolved.

Level 7, Lesson 12, Review of lessons 7-11

Lesson 12 Review Day 5

Review of words with the f sound using f, ff, ph, and gh

List Words

pharmacy	effective	microphone	fragile
rougher	baffled	emphatic	future
triumph	suffocate	autograph	favorite
pheasant	raffle	facility	fantastic
	affiliate	farrier	

A. Unscramble the following list words.

aifflatie

1. _____

frarire

2. _____

flacyiit

3. _____

ftaantsic

4. _____

tirmuhp

5. _____

fraivote

6. _____

eefftcive

7. _____

fblafed

8. _____

hpmaracy

9. _____

rmipcoheon

10. _____

fgirale

11. _____

pehmatic

12. _____

rgourhe

13. _____

ufrute

14. _____

usoffceat

15. _____

aoguatrph

16. _____

frlafe

17. _____

ephaasnt

18. _____

B. Write the definition from Day 1 for the list word **fragile**.

_____

_____

_____

Level 7, Lesson 12, Review of lessons 7-11

<<Intentionally left blank>>

Lesson 13 Day 1

Words with **geo**, **act**, **bio**, **port**, and **graph**

1. **Review Your List Words**
   Look at the list words below and read each word to yourself. Then review each definition.

List Words/Definitions

Word	Definition
biology *biology*	The scientific study of living things.
biography *biography*	A written history of someone's life.
antibiotic *antibiotic*	A substance made from bacteria and used in prevention and treatment of serious diseases.
surgeon *surgeon*	A physician who performs operations.
courageous *courageous*	To be brave in the face of danger.
dungeon *dungeon*	A dark underground prison.
geologist *geologist*	One who studies rocks and the earth's formation.
gorgeous *gorgeous*	Beautiful or attractive.
abstract *abstract*	A summary of something.
activate *activate*	To place something into action.
artifact *artifact*	A man-made object of historical or archaeological interest.
extract *extract*	To pull out or remove.
important *important*	Having much relevancy.
deport *deport*	To expel or send away from a country.
passport *passport*	A government document that allows a citizen to leave his country.
choreograph *choreograph*	To compose a dance routine to music.
paragraph *paragraph*	More than one sentence used together to form a topic or thought.
seismograph *seismograph*	A device used to measure the intensity and duration of an earthquake.

2. **Take Your Pretest**
   Turn to the next page to the Pretest section and your teacher will ask you to write each list word one at a time.

Level 7, Lesson 13 – Words with **geo**, **act**, **bio**, **port**, and **graph**

Date: _____

Pretest - Lesson 13: **Correction Area:**

1. _____ _____
2. _____ _____
3. _____ _____
4. _____ _____
5. _____ _____
6. _____ _____
7. _____ _____
8. _____ _____
9. _____ _____
10. _____ _____
11. _____ _____
12. _____ _____
13. _____ _____
14. _____ _____
15. _____ _____
16. _____ _____
17. _____ _____
18. _____ _____

Carry-over Words: **Correction Area:**

1. _____ _____
2. _____ _____
3. _____ _____
4. _____ _____

Level 7, Lesson 13 – Words with **geo**, **act**, **bio**, **port**, and **graph**

Lesson 13
Day 2

biology	courageous	activate	passport
biography	dungeon	artifact	choreograph
antibiotic	geologist	extract	paragraph
surgeon	gorgeous	important	seismograph
	abstract	deport	

A. Finish the crossword puzzle.

Across:
1. Brave.
5. A man-made object.
7. One who performs operations.
8. Expel from the country.
9. Beautiful or attractive.
11. Prevents serious disease.
14. One who studies rocks.
15. Allows you to travel outside of your country.
16. History of someone's life.
17. More than one sentence.

Down:
1. To compose a dance routine.
2. To make active.
3. A dark underground prison.
4. To pull out.
6. A summary.
10. Measures earthquakes.
12. Study of life.
13. Having much relevancy.

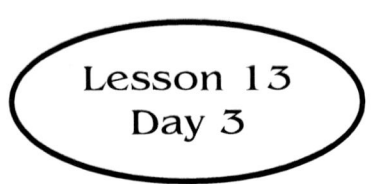

Date: _____

biology	courageous	activate	passport
biography	dungeon	artifact	choreograph
antibiotic	geologist	extract	paragraph
surgeon	gorgeous	important	seismograph
	abstract	deport	

A. **Proofreading.** Underline any words that are misspelled. Insert **punctuation** where needed. Mark an **X** through any letters that are incorrectly **capitalized** or through any incorrect **punctuation**. Circle any letters that should be **capitalized** but are not. Correctly write the list words in the order they appear in the below paragraphs.

the scientist who studied bilogy invented a new type of important antibeotic which also helped the body extracte and actevate additional white blood cells? it was a curageous, undertaking as all the other Scientists in the field said that it could not be done. There was one surgun who believed it was possible and wrote an abstrack on the topic.

1. _____ 2. _____ 3. _____

4. _____ 5. _____ 6. _____

7. _____ 8. _____

This parugraff is about a gorjous geolujist who found an artafact in a dunjun in France? she placed a sizemograph there to measure any earthquake activity. france was threatening to deeport her since she did not have her pasport. there, is talk about someone wanting to write a biografy about her

9. _____ 10. _____ 11. _____

12. _____ 13. _____ 14. _____

15. _____ 16. _____ 17. _____

B. Copy the following sentence. **Stanley wanted to choreograph a dance for the courageous girls by using his favorite song.**

_____

_____

_____

_____

Level 7, Lesson 13 – Words with **geo**, **act**, **bio**, **port**, and **graph**

Date: _____

Lesson 13 Day 4

biology	courageous	activate	passport
biography	dungeon	artifact	choreograph
antibiotic	geologist	extract	paragraph
surgeon	gorgeous	important	seismograph
	abstract	deport	

A. Write the list word that matches each brief definition.

1. More than one sentence.
   _____

2. A physician who operates.
   _____

3. To compose a dance routine to music.
   _____

4. A document that allows travel.
   _____

5. Beautiful or attractive.
   _____

6. One who studies rocks.
   _____

7. To pull out or remove.
   _____

8. A man-made object with historical interest.
   _____

9. A dark underground prison.
   _____

10. Used in prevention and treatment of disease.
    _____

11. To be brave in the face of danger.
    _____

12. To expel one from a country.
    _____

13. Study of living things.
    _____

14. Having much relevancy.
    _____

15. A written history of someone's life.
    _____

16. To place something into action.
    _____

17. A device used to measure earthquakes.
    _____

18. A summary of something.
    _____

B. Write the definition from Day 1 for the list word **seismograph**.

_____

_____

_____

Level 7, Lesson 13 – Words with **geo**, **act**, **bio**, **port**, and **graph**

Date: _____

Lesson 13 - Day 5, Final Test

Correction Area:

1. _____ _____
2. _____ _____
3. _____ _____
4. _____ _____
5. _____ _____
6. _____ _____
7. _____ _____
8. _____ _____
9. _____ _____
10. _____ _____
11. _____ _____
12. _____ _____
13. _____ _____
14. _____ _____
15. _____ _____
16. _____ _____
17. _____ _____
18. _____ _____

Carry-over Words: Correction Area:

1. _____ _____
2. _____ _____
3. _____ _____
4. _____ _____

Level 7, Lesson 13 – Words with **geo**, **act**, **bio**, **port**, and **graph**

Lesson 14 Day 1

Words that mean a type of sound made with the mouth

1. **Review Your List Words**
   Look at the list words below and read each word to yourself. Then review each definition.

List Words/Definitions

Word	Definition
scream *scream*	• A long and loud piercing sound.
whisper *whisper*	• A soft or hushed statement.
demand *demand*	• To require by giving direction.
talk *talk*	• To speak in regular levels and tones.
comment *comment*	• An expression or opinion.
blurt *blurt*	• A quick comment made without much thought.
explain *explain*	• To make a clarifying statement.
reply *reply*	• A response to a question.
remark *remark*	• To make a short comment based upon an observation.
inquire *inquire*	• To ask for information with a question.
ask *ask*	• To put a question to.
question *question*	• An expression of inquiry that requires a response.
whine *whine*	• A loud, high-pitched cry or moan.
mention *mention*	• To speak briefly about something.
advise *advise*	• To provide guidance.
insist *insist*	• To place great stress or importance upon a statement.
rebuff *rebuff*	• To criticize or refuse.
exclaim *exclaim*	• To cry out with strong emotion.

2. **Take Your Pretest**
   Turn to the next page to the Pretest section and your teacher will ask you to write each list word one at a time.

Date: _____

Pretest - Lesson 14: **Correction Area:**

1. _____   _____
2. _____   _____
3. _____   _____
4. _____   _____
5. _____   _____
6. _____   _____
7. _____   _____
8. _____   _____
9. _____   _____
10. _____   _____
11. _____   _____
12. _____   _____
13. _____   _____
14. _____   _____
15. _____   _____
16. _____   _____
17. _____   _____
18. _____   _____

Carry-over Words: **Correction Area:**

1. _____   _____
2. _____   _____
3. _____   _____
4. _____   _____

Level 7, Lesson 14 – Words that mean a type of sound made with the mouth

Date: _____

Lesson 14 Day 2

scream	comment	inquire	advise
whisper	blurt	ask	insist
demand	explain	question	rebuff
talk	reply	whine	exclaim
	remark	mention	

A. Write the list word in the blanks that answers each clue. Read down the shaded row to find the answer to the question asked. Write the answer to the question in the spaces provided.

1. A long and loud piercing sound.
2. An expression or opinion.
4. Response to a question.
5. A loud, high-pitched cry or moan.
6. To place great importance on a statement.
7. Cry out with strong emotion.
8. A soft hushed voice.
9. A clarifying statement.
10. To speak in a normal voice.
11. To criticize or refuse.

"Bobby thought about going to work at the glass factory where mirrors are made, but somehow he just couldn't _____ working there."

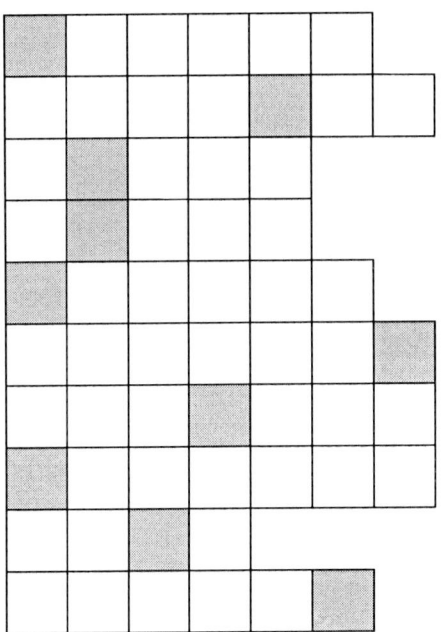

Answer:

___ ___ ___   ___ ___ ___ ___ ___ ___ ___

B. Write a short paragraph below using at least four list words.

_____

_____

_____

_____

_____

Level 7, Lesson 14 – Words that mean a type of sound made with the mouth

Date: _____

scream	comment	inquire	advise
whisper	blurt	ask	insist
demand	explain	question	rebuff
talk	reply	whine	exclaim
	remark	mention	

A. Unscramble the following list words.

mrreak
1. _____

nmteion
2. _____

iwhpser
3. _____

epaxlin
4. _____

eacxlim
5. _____

sinist
6. _____

rsacem
7. _____

hiwne
8. _____

mcenomt
9. _____

asdive
10. _____

sak
11. _____

rffebu
12. _____

qiinure
13. _____

lbtur
14. _____

ryepl
15. _____

klta
16. _____

stqueion
17. _____

ddeamn
18. _____

B. Write the definition from Day 1 for the list word **remark**.

_____

_____

Level 7, Lesson 14 – Words that mean a type of sound made with the mouth

Lesson 14 Day 4

scream	comment	inquire	advise
whisper	blurt	ask	insist
demand	explain	question	rebuff
talk	reply	whine	exclaim
	remark	mention	

A. Write each group of three list words in alphabetical order.

reply, remark, rebuff

1. _____ 2. _____ 3. _____

ask, advise, blurt

4. _____ 5. _____ 6. _____

demand, question, exclaim

7. _____ 8. _____ 9. _____

scream, comment, talk

10. _____ 11. _____ 12. _____

mention, whine, inquire

13. _____ 14. _____ 15. _____

whisper, ask, insist

16. _____ 17. _____ 18. _____

scream, explain, insist

19. _____ 20. _____ 21. _____

demand, reply, exclaim

22. _____ 23. _____ 24. _____

whisper, whine, talk

25. _____ 26. _____ 27. _____

remark, advise, comment

28. _____ 29. _____ 30. _____

Level 7, Lesson 14 – Words that mean a type of sound made with the mouth

Date: _____

Lesson 14 - Day 5, Final Test

Correction Area:

1. _____
2. _____
3. _____
4. _____
5. _____
6. _____
7. _____
8. _____
9. _____
10. _____
11. _____
12. _____
13. _____
14. _____
15. _____
16. _____
17. _____
18. _____

Carry-over Words:

Correction Area:

1. _____
2. _____
3. _____
4. _____

Level 7, Lesson 14 – Words that mean a type of sound made with the mouth

Date: _____

Words with prefixes mis and anti

1. **Review Your List Words**
Look at the list words below and read each word to yourself. Then review each definition.

The prefix **anti** can mean **against** or **opposite of/to**.

The prefix **mis** means **bad**, **failure**, or **wrong**.

List Words/Definitions

Word	Definition	Word	Definition
antibacterial *antibacterial*	Any drug that works against and kills bacteria.	**misbehave** *misbehave*	Not behaving properly. Behaving wrongly.
antibodies *antibodies*	Proteins found in blood cells that work against and kill bacteria.	**misprint** *misprint*	An incorrect or bad printing of something.
anticlimax *anticlimax*	A disappointing decline after a rise. Opposite of climax.	**mismatched** *mismatched*	Something that is not matched or matched wrongly.
anticompetitive *anticompetitive*	Something that is bad for competition. Against competition.	**misplaced** *misplaced*	Something that is lost or placed wrongly.
antithesis *antithesis*	The exact opposite of something.	**misguided** *misguided*	Having incorrect or bad views or ideas.
antifreeze *antifreeze*	A liquid that works against and prohibits freezing.	**misleading** *misleading*	To deceive or trick someone by providing bad information.
antidote *antidote*	Something that works against and reverses the effect of poison.	**mismanaged** *mismanaged*	To not take care when handling one's affairs. Manage wrongly.
antiperspirant *antiperspirant*	Something that works against and stops perspiration.	**misspoken** *misspoken*	To say something that is incorrect. Spoken wrongly.
antisocial *antisocial*	Someone or something that is unfriendly. The opposite of social.	**misstep** *misstep*	A mistake or to take a bad or wrong step.

2. **Take Your Pretest**
Turn to the next page to the Pretest section and your teacher will ask you to write each list word one at a time.

Date: _____

Pretest - Lesson 15:   Correction Area:

1. _____ _____
2. _____ _____
3. _____ _____
4. _____ _____
5. _____ _____
6. _____ _____
7. _____ _____
8. _____ _____
9. _____ _____
10. _____ _____
11. _____ _____
12. _____ _____
13. _____ _____
14. _____ _____
15. _____ _____
16. _____ _____
17. _____ _____
18. _____ _____

Carry-over Words: Correction Area:

1. _____ _____
2. _____ _____
3. _____ _____
4. _____ _____

Level 7, Lesson 15 – Words with prefixes **mis** and **anti**

Date: _____

antibacterial	antithesis	misbehave	misleading
antibodies	antifreeze	misprint	mismanaged
anticlimax	antidote	mismatched	misspoken
anticompetitive	antiperspirant	misplaced	misstep
	antisocial	misguided	

A. Finish the crossword puzzle.

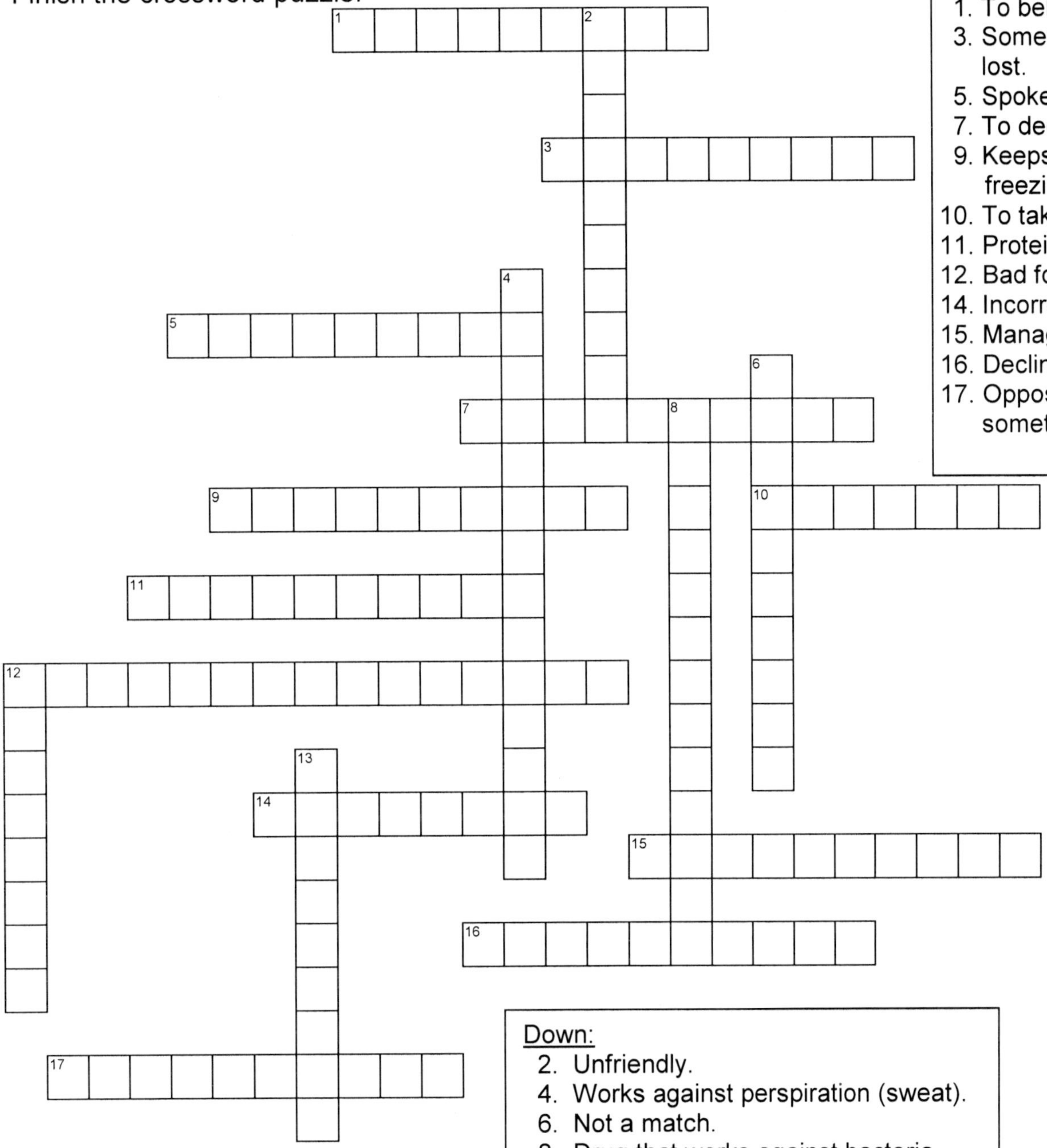

Across:
1. To behave wrongly.
3. Something that is lost.
5. Spoken wrongly.
7. To deceive.
9. Keeps from freezing.
10. To take a bad step.
11. Protein kills germs.
12. Bad for competition.
14. Incorrect print.
15. Managed wrongly.
16. Decline after rise.
17. Opposite of something.

Down:
2. Unfriendly.
4. Works against perspiration (sweat).
6. Not a match.
8. Drug that works against bacteria.
12. Works against and reverses effects of poison.
13. Incorrect or bad views or ideas.

Level 7, Lesson 15 – Words with prefixes **mis** and **anti**

Lesson 15 Day 3

Date: _____

antibacterial	antithesis	misbehave	misleading
antibodies	antifreeze	misprint	mismanaged
anticlimax	antidote	mismatched	misspoken
anticompetitive	antiperspirant	misplaced	misstep
	antisocial	misguided	

A. Read the following paragraph and write in the lines below the list words you see.

   The antisocial doctor had misspoken when he said the antibacterial antibodies worked as an antidote to the poison. Apparently, there was a misprint in the medical journal that was misleading and resulted in a misguided treatment plan.

1. _____   2. _____

3. _____   4. _____

5. _____   6. _____

7. _____   8. _____

   Terri misplaced her antiperspirant and wore mismatched socks because of a mismanaged laundry process. For some reason this made her take a misstep which was the antithesis of her personality. When Terri was sweaty, she also tended to misbehave.

9. _____   10. _____

11. _____   12. _____

13. _____   14. _____

15. _____

   By Tom not using antifreeze in his radiator during the winter race, it made for an anticompetitive race and the finish was an anticlimax since we had all hoped for a close finish.

16. _____   17. _____

18. _____

B. Write the definition from Day 1 for the list word **mismanaged**.

_____

_____

_____

Level 7, Lesson 15 – Words with prefixes **mis** and **anti**

Date: _____

Lesson 15 Day 4

antibacterial	antithesis	misbehave	misleading
antibodies	antifreeze	misprint	mismanaged
anticlimax	antidote	mismatched	misspoken
anticompetitive	antiperspirant	misplaced	misstep
	antisocial	misguided	

A. Find and circle each list word in the puzzle below.

```
A Z A A L Y D E C A L P S I M
N P N N H A T V P D G M D G A
T D T T A N T I B O D I E S L
I E I I S T X T V A I S H E Y
F G C P D I Z I U N C S C V G
R A L E E S S T N N U P T A N
E N I R D O M E G M K O A H I
E A M S I C I P H W C K M E D
Z M A P U I S M S T C E S B A
E S X I G A P O I Z I N I S E
A I O R S L R C T S V T M I L
D M F A I E I I V S S G N M S
V N O N M A N T I D O T E A I
V T C T G Z T N B D Q L E X M
L A I R E T C A B I T N A P C
```

B. Copy the following sentence. **Harold was often misspoken and misleading and as a result became antisocial.**

_____

_____

_____

_____

Level 7, Lesson 15 – Words with prefixes **mis** and **anti**

Lesson 15 - Day 5, Final Test

Date: _____

Correction Area:

1. _____
2. _____
3. _____
4. _____
5. _____
6. _____
7. _____
8. _____
9. _____
10. _____
11. _____
12. _____
13. _____
14. _____
15. _____
16. _____
17. _____
18. _____

Carry-over Words:

Correction Area:

1. _____
2. _____
3. _____
4. _____

Level 7, Lesson 15 – Words with prefixes **mis** and **anti**

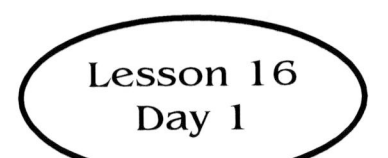

Date: _____

Words with **con** and **non**

1. **Review Your List Words**
   Look at the list words below and read each word to yourself. Then review each definition.

List Words/Definitions

concur	nonsense
• To agree.	• Foolish or meaningless words.
concurrent	**nonexistent**
• Happen at the same time as something else.	• Something that does not exist.
condensate	**nonfiction**
• To condense into a liquid form.	• Writings that are not pretend.
condone	**nontoxic**
• To overlook or forgive.	• Something that is not toxic or poisonous.
conduct	**nonstop**
• To lead or guide. Also, to transmit heat, light, sound, or electricity.	• Something that continues on and does not stop.
configure	**nonprofit**
• To arrange in a certain form or shape.	• An entity that is not run for the primary purpose of making a profit.
construct	**nonflammable**
• To build.	• A substance that is not flammable.
confirm	**nondescript**
• To provide a formal acknowledgement.	• Something that does not have any distinct features.
conjoined	**nonchalant**
• Separate entities joined together.	• Having a carefree attitude toward something.

2. **Take Your Pretest**
   Turn to the next page to the Pretest section and your teacher will ask you to write each list word one at a time.

Date: _____

Pretest - Lesson 16:   Correction Area:

1. _____ _____
2. _____ _____
3. _____ _____
4. _____ _____
5. _____ _____
6. _____ _____
7. _____ _____
8. _____ _____
9. _____ _____
10. _____ _____
11. _____ _____
12. _____ _____
13. _____ _____
14. _____ _____
15. _____ _____
16. _____ _____
17. _____ _____
18. _____ _____

Carry-over Words: Correction Area:

1. _____ _____
2. _____ _____
3. _____ _____
4. _____ _____

Level 7, Lesson 16 – Words with **con** and **non**

Date: _____

Lesson 16
Day 2

concur	conduct	nonsense	nonprofit
concurrent	configure	nonexistent	nonflammable
condensate	construct	nonfiction	nondescript
condone	confirm	nontoxic	nonchalant
	conjoined	nonstop	

A. Cross out the word that is spelled incorrectly. Write the correctly spelled words on the lines.

1. (concer, concur) _____
2. (configure, configur) _____
3. (nonexistant, nonexistent) _____
4. (nonstop, nonestop) _____
5. (nonprophet, nonprofit) _____
6. (conndone, condone) _____
7. (nonsense, nonscense) _____
8. (nonflammable, nonflamable) _____
9. (condensate, condensaite) _____
10. (concurent, concurrent) _____
11. (conduct, conducte) _____
12. (nonfician, nonfiction) _____
13. (nonchallant, nonchalant) _____
14. (conjoined, conjoind) _____
15. (construct, cunstruct) _____
16. (nondescript, nondescrip) _____
17. (confirme, confirm) _____
18. (nontocksick, nontoxic) _____

B. Write the definition from Day 1 for the list word **conjoined**.

_____

_____

_____

Level 7, Lesson 16 – Words with **con** and **non**   93

Lesson 16 Day 3

Date: _____

concur	conduct	nonsense	nonprofit
concurrent	configure	nonexistent	nonflammable
condensate	construct	nonfiction	nondescript
condone	confirm	nontoxic	nonchalant
	conjoined	nonstop	

A. Use the following code to finish the sentences.

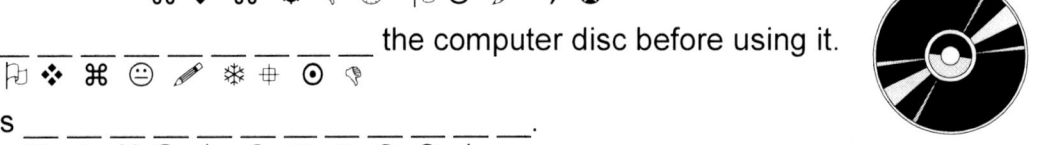

1. The boss did not __condone__ the __conduct__ of his employees.
2. The paint can says that the paint is __nontoxic__.
3. The humid air started to __condensate__ on the window.
4. Doyle had a __nonchalant__ attitude while cleaning his room.
5. Her brown car was very __nondescript__.
6. Betsy had to __configure__ the computer disc before using it.
7. The water was __nonflammable__.
8. I had to __concur__ that spring break was not a good time to go on vacation.
9. I watched television and read a book in a __concurrent__ manner.
10. Jeffrey got excited and started talking __nonstop__.
11. Fish in the old lake were __nonexistent__.
12. The two computers were __conjoined__ in order to handle the traffic.
13. The story about building skyscrapers was a book of __nonfiction__.
14. Janet kept talking __nonsense__.
15. Toby needed to __construct__ a house large enough for his family.
16. The hotel needed to __confirm__ our reservation.
17. The hospital operated as a __nonprofit__.

Level 7, Lesson 16 – Words with **con** and **non**

Lesson 16 Day 4

Date: _____

concur	conduct	nonsense	nonprofit
concurrent	configure	nonexistent	nonflammable
condensate	construct	nonfiction	nondescript
condone	confirm	nontoxic	nonchalant
	conjoined	nonstop	

A. Find and circle each list word in the puzzle below.

```
P O T S N O N S J J B P T N E
N O N T O X I C A Y P L N O O
T N E T S I X E N O N O E N D
Q P R T E N S K C T N E R P E
B N I M O N U O A F T C R R N
K X J R E N N R L A O O U O I
P D C S C F O A S N W N C F O
Y R N O I S M N F I M D N I J
M O U G N M E I C L J O O T N
N A U C A D R D E H S N C Q O
F R M B N M U F N F A E K R C
E T L O J O V C X O V L G N C
J E C I F J C Y T Q N G A N X
T F Z N O N F I C T I O N N W
I L S N T C U R T S N O C U T
```

B. Copy the following sentence. **The patient did not condone the nonchalant conduct of the surgeon as he began his surgery.**

_____

_____

_____

_____

Level 7, Lesson 16 – Words with **con** and **non**

Lesson 16 - Day 5, Final Test

Date: _____

Correction Area:

1. _____
2. _____
3. _____
4. _____
5. _____
6. _____
7. _____
8. _____
9. _____
10. _____
11. _____
12. _____
13. _____
14. _____
15. _____
16. _____
17. _____
18. _____

Carry-over Words:

Correction Area:

1. _____
2. _____
3. _____
4. _____

Level 7, Lesson 16 – Words with **con** and **non**

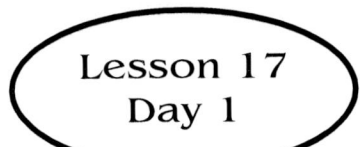

Words that mean **to move**

1. **Review Your List Words**
   Look at the list words below and read each word to yourself. Then review each definition.

List Words/Definitions

travel *travel*	climbing *climbing*
• To journey from one place to another.	• Moving upward.
migrate *migrate*	**swimming** *swimming*
• To move from one country to another.	• Moving through water.
proceed *proceed*	**roaming** *roaming*
• To move forward or onward.	• Moving around with no purpose.
relocate *relocate*	**transport** *transport*
• To become established in a new area.	• To carry something from one place to another.
leave *leave*	**bustle** *bustle*
• To exit or go away.	• To move about in a noisy manner.
sprint *sprint*	**bicycling** *bicycling*
• Run quickly for a short distance.	• Moving about on a bicycle.
gallop *gallop*	**mobile** *mobile*
• A fast way for a four-footed animal to run.	• Easily moved.
transfer *transfer*	**transit** *transit*
• To pass from one person, place, or thing to another.	• Moving passengers or goods.
traverse *traverse*	**rotate** *rotate*
• To pass across, over, or through something.	• To move in a twisting or circular fashion.

2. **Take Your Pretest**
   Turn to the next page to the Pretest section and your teacher will ask you to write each list word one at a time.

Date: _____

Pretest - Lesson 17: Correction Area:

1. _____ _____
2. _____ _____
3. _____ _____
4. _____ _____
5. _____ _____
6. _____ _____
7. _____ _____
8. _____ _____
9. _____ _____
10. _____ _____
11. _____ _____
12. _____ _____
13. _____ _____
14. _____ _____
15. _____ _____
16. _____ _____
17. _____ _____
18. _____ _____

Carry-over Words: Correction Area:

1. _____ _____
2. _____ _____
3. _____ _____
4. _____ _____

Level 7, Lesson 17 – Words that mean **to move**

Date: _____

Lesson 17 Day 2

travel	leave	climbing	bicycling
migrate	sprint	swimming	mobile
proceed	gallop	roaming	transit
relocate	transfer	transport	rotate
	traverse	bustle	

A. Read each clue. Write the list word in the blanks that answers the given clue. Read down the shaded row to find the answer to the question asked. Write the answer to the question in the space provided. Look in a thesaurus if you need help.

1. Riding a bicycle.
2. Moving passengers or goods.
3. A fast way for a four-footed animal to run.
4. Pass from one person to another.
5. To twist.
6. Moving through the water.
7. To journey from one place to another.
8. To move to another country.
9. Easily moved.
10. Get established in a new place.
11. To move forward.

"Why did the chicken refuse to cross the road? Because he was _____."

Answer:

___ ___   ___   ___ ___ ___ ___   ___ ___ ___ ___ .

B. Copy the following sentence. **Barry wanted to traverse the mountain in order to get away from the hustle and bustle of the city.**

_____

_____

_____

_____

Level 7, Lesson 17 – Words that mean **to move**   99

Date: _____

travel	leave	climbing	bicycling
migrate	sprint	swimming	mobile
proceed	gallop	roaming	transit
relocate	transfer	transport	rotate
	traverse	bustle	

A. Write each group of three list words in alphabetical order.

traverse, transfer, travel

1. _____ 2. _____ 3. _____

transit, transport, traverse

4. _____ 5. _____ 6. _____

rotate, relocate, roaming

7. _____ 8. _____ 9. _____

bustle, climbing, bicycling

10. _____ 11. _____ 12. _____

mobile, leave, migrate

13. _____ 14. _____ 15. _____

swimming, proceed, sprint

16. _____ 17. _____ 18. _____

proceed, rotate, gallop

19. _____ 20. _____ 21. _____

leave, gallop, bicycling

22. _____ 23. _____ 24. _____

transit, transfer, travel

25. _____ 26. _____ 27. _____

sprint, migrate, bustle

28. _____ 29. _____ 30. _____

Level 7, Lesson 17 – Words that mean **to move**

Date: _____

travel	leave	climbing	bicycling
migrate	sprint	swimming	mobile
proceed	gallop	roaming	transit
relocate	transfer	transport	rotate
	traverse	bustle	

A. Draw a line to connect each list word with its definition.

travel	To move forward or onward.
migrate	To carry something from one place to another.
proceed	Moving passengers or goods.
relocate	Easily moved.
leave	Moving around with no purpose.
sprint	To move from one country to another.
gallop	Moving about on a bicycle.
transfer	To pass from one person to another.
transverse	To pass across, over, or through something.
climbing	To move in a twisting or circular fashion.
swimming	A fast way for a four-footed animal to run.
roaming	To move about in a noisy manner.
transport	Moving upward.
bustle	To exit or go away.
bicycling	To journey from one place to another.
mobile	To become established in a new area.
transit	Run quickly for a short distance.
rotate	Moving through water.

B. Write the definition from Day 1 for the list word **relocate**.

_____

_____

_____

Level 7, Lesson 17 – Words that mean **to move**

Lesson 17 - Day 5, Final Test

Date: _____

Correction Area:

1. _____
2. _____
3. _____
4. _____
5. _____
6. _____
7. _____
8. _____
9. _____
10. _____
11. _____
12. _____
13. _____
14. _____
15. _____
16. _____
17. _____
18. _____

Carry-over Words:

Correction Area:

1. _____
2. _____
3. _____
4. _____

Level 7, Lesson 17 – Words that mean **to move**

Lesson 18 Review Day 1

Review of words with geo, act, bio, port, and graph

List Words

biology	courageous	activate	passport
biography	dungeon	artifact	choreograph
antibiotic	geologist	extract	paragraph
surgeon	gorgeous	important	seismograph
	abstract	deport	

A. Find and circle each list word in the puzzle below.

Level 7, Lesson 18, Review of lessons 13-17

Date: _____

Lesson 18 Review Day 2

Review of words that mean a type of sound made with the mouth

List Words

scream	comment	inquire	advise
whisper	blurt	ask	insist
demand	explain	question	rebuff
talk	reply	whine	exclaim
	remark	mention	

A. Write the list word that matches each brief definition.

1. A loud, high-pitched cry or moan. _____

2. To criticize or refuse. _____

3. To place great importance on a statement. _____

4. To speak briefly about something. _____

5. To cry out with strong emotion. _____

6. To make a short comment based upon an observation. _____

7. A response to a question. _____

8. A long and loud piercing sound. _____

9. To make a clarifying statement. _____

10. An expression or opinion. _____

11. To require by giving direction. _____

12. A quick comment without thought. _____

13. A soft or hushed statement. _____

14. To put a question to. _____

15. To provide guidance. _____

16. An expression of inquiry that requires a response. _____

17. To speak in regular levels and tones. _____

18. A question asking for information. _____

Level 7, Lesson 18, Review of lessons 13-17

Lesson 18 Review Day 3

Review of words with prefixes **mis** and **anti**

List Words

antibacterial	antithesis	misbehave	misleading
antibodies	antifreeze	misprint	mismanaged
anticlimax	antidote	mismatched	misspoken
anticompetitive	antiperspirant	misplaced	misstep
	antisocial	misguided	

A. Use the following code to finish the sentences.

A	B	C	D	E	F	G	H	I	J	K	L	M	N	O	P	Q	R	S	T	U	V	W	X	Y	Z
Ω	☺	⌘	❄	♠	☻	❄	☼	✎	📧	❓	♦	❀	⌘	❖	✈	●	◉	✪	✪	⊕	×	⌛	✒	☎	📖

1. The new soap was _____.
2. The ending of the show was an _____.
3. The article contained a _____ by the new writer.
4. The puppy would constantly _____ when alone.
5. The hobo became _____ after living alone for so long.
6. There was an _____ for the snake poison.
7. You'll need some _____ in your radiator during the winter.
8. Gary _____ his car keys again.
9. Although he meant well, Grandpa's directions were _____.
10. Brian was poor because he _____ his money.
11. The _____ lady said that is was Saturday and not Sunday.
12. Ed needed some _____ to keep dry.
13. The undersized shoes made Ann _____ all over the place.
14. Bob's sales tactics for the used car were _____.
15. The basketball game was _____.
16. The _____ in her blood kept her healthy.
17. The bookends were _____.
18. Tom's personality was the _____ of his twin brother Tim.

Level 7, Lesson 18, Review of lessons 13-17

Lesson 18 Review Day 4

Review of words with **con** and **non**

List Words

concur	conduct	nonsense	nonprofit
concurrent	configure	nonexistent	nonflammable
condensate	construct	nonfiction	nondescript
condone	confirm	nontoxic	nonchalant
	conjoined	nonstop	

A. Unscramble the following list words.

cjoinoned

1. _____

ntopnso

2. _____

cnoonde

3. _____

nohcnalant

4. _____

pnronofit

5. _____

sneonnse

6. _____

ccounr

7. _____

ctonudc

8. _____

ccournrent

9. _____

ctornsuct

10. _____

fnoanlmmable

11. _____

cofinrm

12. _____

cognifure

13. _____

enosxnitent

14. _____

cdoennsate

15. _____

nocdensript

16. _____

noxontic

17. _____

nofniicton

18. _____

Lesson 18 Review Day 5

Review of words that mean to move

List Words

travel	leave	climbing	bicycling
migrate	sprint	swimming	mobile
proceed	gallop	roaming	transit
relocate	transfer	transport	rotate
	traverse	bustle	

A. **Guide words** are placed at the top of each page of a dictionary to provide an alphabetical guide for finding entry words that appear on that page. For example, assume that a page has the guide words **fast** and **feline**. The entry word **farmer** would **not** be found on that page because alphabetically it does not fall between these guide words. On the other hand, the entry word **feeling** would be found on that page.

Look at each pair of guide words, then write the list word on the line that would appear on the dictionary page.

1. bush — busy _____
2. rot — rotten _____
3. swill — swing _____
4. trash — traveling _____
5. travelogue — trawler _____
6. transcribe — transform _____
7. transplant — transpose _____
8. transient — translate _____
9. relive — rely _____
10. leather — lecture _____
11. spring — sprite _____
12. galley — gamble _____
13. mob — mock _____
14. problem — process _____
15. road — roar _____
16. click — clinch _____
17. biceps — bid _____
18. might — mile _____

Level 7, Lesson 18, Review of lessons 13-17

Date: _____

Words that have to do with feelings or emotions

1. **Review Your List Words**
   Look at the list words below and read each word to yourself. Then review each definition.

List Words/Definitions

beautiful *beautiful* • Visually pleasing. A delight to the senses.		**frightened** *frightened* • To be scared.	
patient *patient* • A showing of calmness.		**confident** *confident* • To believe strongly in oneself.	
disgusted *disgusted* • A strong dislike for something.		**distracted** *distracted* • Showing a lack of attention.	
infuriated *infuriated* • To be angry or enraged.		**helplessness** *helplessness* • A feeling of being unable to help oneself.	
complacent *complacent* • To be satisfied.		**depressed** *depressed* • To be in a saddened state.	
ecstatic *ecstatic* • To be excited.		**sleepy** *sleepy* • To be tired and in need of sleep.	
hopeful *hopeful* • To look forward to something.		**rested** *rested* • To have been relaxing or inactive. To be at peace or ease.	
exhausted *exhausted* • To be drained of energy. Weary.		**compassionate** *compassionate* • To have a desire to help someone. Sympathetic.	
apprehensive *apprehensive* • To be fearful of the future.		**enthusiastic** *enthusiastic* • Showing great excitement and interest.	

2. **Take Your Pretest**
   Turn to the next page to the Pretest section and your teacher will ask you to write each list word one at a time.

Date: _____

Pretest - Lesson 19: **Correction Area:**

1. _____ _____
2. _____ _____
3. _____ _____
4. _____ _____
5. _____ _____
6. _____ _____
7. _____ _____
8. _____ _____
9. _____ _____
10. _____ _____
11. _____ _____
12. _____ _____
13. _____ _____
14. _____ _____
15. _____ _____
16. _____ _____
17. _____ _____
18. _____ _____

Carry-over Words: **Correction Area:**

1. _____ _____
2. _____ _____
3. _____ _____
4. _____ _____

Level 7, Lesson 19 – Words that have to do with **feelings** or **emotions**

beautiful	complacent	frightened	sleepy
patient	ecstatic	confident	rested
disgusted	hopeful	distracted	compassionate
infuriated	exhausted	helplessness	enthusiastic
	apprehensive	depressed	

A. Cross out the word that is spelled incorrectly. Write the correctly spelled words on the lines.

1. (aprenhenssive, apprehensive) _____
2. (depresed, depressed) _____
3. (sleepy, sleepey) _____
4. (beautiful, beutiful) _____
5. (eccstatic, ecstatic) _____
6. (hopeful, hopefull) _____
7. (fritened, frightened) _____
8. (compasiontate, compassionate) _____
9. (patiece, patient) _____
10. (infuriated, infurriated) _____
11. (disgusted, disgussted) _____
12. (helplessness, helplesnes) _____
13. (enthusiastic, enthisiastic) _____
14. (disttracted, distracted) _____
15. (rested, restide) _____
16. (complacent, complacant) _____
17. (exsausted, exhausted) _____
18. (confedent, confident) _____

B. Write the definition from Day 1 for the list word **distracted**.

_____

_____

_____

Level 7, Lesson 19 – Words that have to do with **feelings** or **emotions**

Date: _____

beautiful	complacent	frightened	sleepy
patient	ecstatic	confident	rested
disgusted	hopeful	distracted	compassionate
infuriated	exhausted	helplessness	enthusiastic
	apprehensive	depressed	

A. Write the list words that complete each sentence. A hint word is given.

1. Avery was (dislike) _____ by the piles of rotten garbage.
2. Mary was (lack of attention) _____ by the radio playing while reading.
3. His boss was (angry) _____ with the lack of work.
4. Doug was (scared) _____ by the spider hanging by his head.
5. The picture she drew was (visually pleasing) _____.
6. Rod was (looking forward) _____ that he could solve the problem.
7. Jodi was (excited) _____ about learning a new cheer.
8. Tom was (great excitement) _____ in cheering for his team.
9. Doris was (calmness) _____ as she waited for a bus.
10. Brad was (weary) _____ after working 12 hours straight.
11. Stewart was (satisfied) _____ after eating a large meal.
12. Gary was (fearful) _____ about receiving his grade in science.
13. Gary was (saddened) _____ after receiving his grade.
14. Ginger was (sure) _____ that she could jump the highest.
15. John was well (inactive) _____ after his nap.
16. His (unable to help oneself) _____ stopped him from building the shed.
17. The baby was (tired) _____ after eating lunch.
18. Beth was (sympathy) _____ towards the weary traveler

B. Copy the following sentence. **Beautiful Beverly was confident and ecstatic that she could complete the race without being exhausted.**

_____

_____

_____

_____

Level 7, Lesson 19 – Words that have to do with **feelings** or **emotions**

Date: _____

Lesson 19
Day 4

beautiful	complacent	frightened	sleepy
patient	ecstatic	confident	rested
disgusted	hopeful	distracted	compassionate
infuriated	exhausted	helplessness	enthusiastic
	apprehensive	depressed	

A. Find and circle each list word in the puzzle below.

```
H  D  B  J  D  P  H  G  I  C  K  A  S  Z  D
C  E  E  E  W  E  O  O  I  V  P  N  L  A  E
O  S  L  N  A  C  T  T  P  P  L  L  E  G  T
N  S  M  P  E  U  A  S  R  E  G  E  E  E  C
F  E  V  Z  L  T  T  E  U  M  F  T  P  N  A
I  R  R  T  S  E  H  I  H  A  B  U  Y  T  R
D  P  Q  C  O  E  S  G  F  I  H  X  L  H  T
E  E  E  P  N  N  B  S  I  U  J  X  M  U  S
N  D  E  S  O  T  V  W  N  R  L  P  E  S  I
T  J  I  B  I  W  R  X  M  E  F  M  Z  I  D
A  V  M  S  D  E  T  S  U  G  S  I  D  A  V
E  T  N  E  C  A  L  P  M  O  C  S  V  S  B
P  A  T  I  E  N  T  D  E  T  S  E  R  T  D
C  O  M  P  A  S  S  I  O  N  A  T  E  I  G
I  N  F  U  R  I  A  T  E  D  S  E  T  C  U
```

B. Write a short paragraph below using at least four list words.

_____

_____

_____

_____

Level 7, Lesson 19 – Words that have to do with **feelings** or **emotions**

Lesson 19 - Day 5, Final Test

Date: _____

Correction Area:

1. _____
2. _____
3. _____
4. _____
5. _____
6. _____
7. _____
8. _____
9. _____
10. _____
11. _____
12. _____
13. _____
14. _____
15. _____
16. _____
17. _____
18. _____

Carry-over Words:

Correction Area:

1. _____
2. _____
3. _____
4. _____

Level 7, Lesson 19 – Words that have to do with **feelings** or **emotions**

Words with **ar**, **are**, **or**, and **ore**

1. **Review Your List Words**
   Look at the list words below and read each word to yourself. Then review each definition.

List Words/Definitions

pardon *pardon* • To forgive or set free from further legal punishment.		**abnormal** *abnormal* • Something that is not normal.	
garden *garden* • A portion of ground where plants are grown for the food they bear.		**advisor** *advisor* • One who provides guidance or advice.	
startle *startle* • To surprise someone or something.		**adorable** *adorable* • Something that is cute or charming.	
sparkle *sparkle* • An object that emits sparks or reflects flashes of light.		**fedora** *fedora* • A hat made of felt with a brim and a creased crown.	
nightmare *nightmare* • A scary dream.		**storage** *storage* • A place where items not being used are housed.	
silverware *silverware* • Utensils used to eat food.		**unforeseen** *unforeseen* • Something that is not anticipated.	
software *software* • Computer readable code used with a computer system.		**carnivore** *carnivore* • Something that feeds on meat.	
unaware *unaware* • Not aware or cognizant.		**boredom** *boredom* • The state of being bored, which means being uninterested.	
ensnare *ensnare* • To trap or capture.		**fluorescent** *fluorescent* • A bulb which emits light due to it having a fluorescent coating.	

2. **Take Your Pretest**
   Turn to the next page to the Pretest section and your teacher will ask you to write each list word one at a time.

Level 7, Lesson 20 – Words with **ar**, **are**, **or**, and **ore**

Date: _____

Pretest – Lesson 20: Correction Area:

1. _____ _____
2. _____ _____
3. _____ _____
4. _____ _____
5. _____ _____
6. _____ _____
7. _____ _____
8. _____ _____
9. _____ _____
10. _____ _____
11. _____ _____
12. _____ _____
13. _____ _____
14. _____ _____
15. _____ _____
16. _____ _____
17. _____ _____
18. _____ _____

Carry-over Words: Correction Area:

1. _____ _____
2. _____ _____
3. _____ _____
4. _____ _____

Level 7, Lesson 20 – Words with **ar**, **are**, **or**, and **ore**

Lesson 20
Day 2

pardon	nightmare	abnormal	unforeseen
garden	silverware	advisor	carnivore
startle	software	adorable	boredom
sparkle	unaware	fedora	fluorescent
	ensnare	storage	

A. Finish the crossword puzzle.

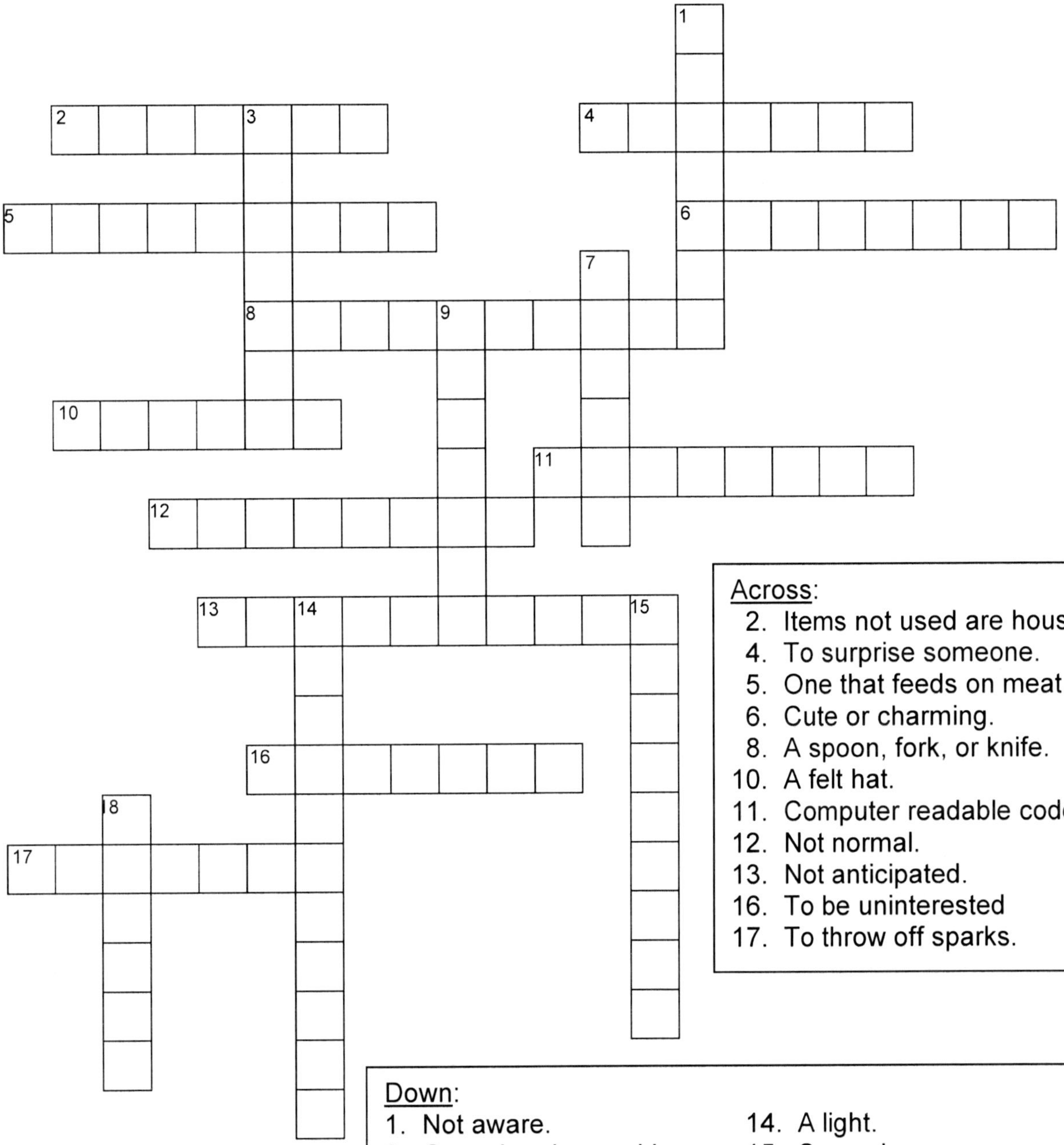

Across:
2. Items not used are housed here.
4. To surprise someone.
5. One that feeds on meat.
6. Cute or charming.
8. A spoon, fork, or knife.
10. A felt hat.
11. Computer readable code.
12. Not normal.
13. Not anticipated.
16. To be uninterested
17. To throw off sparks.

Down:
1. Not aware.
3. One who gives guidance.
7. To forgive.
9. To trap.
14. A light.
15. Scary dream.
18. A place where food is grown.

Level 7, Lesson 20 – Words with **ar**, **are**, **or**, and **ore**   117

Date: _____

Lesson 20 Day 3

pardon	nightmare	abnormal	unforeseen
garden	silverware	advisor	carnivore
startle	software	adorable	boredom
sparkle	unaware	fedora	fluorescent
	ensnare	storage	

A. Write the list words that complete each sentence.

1. Angela used the _____ to eat her lunch.
2. Grandma put the old furniture back into the _____ shed.
3. We watched sunlight _____ on the waves.
4. Lane loves to put a _____ on his head when he goes to dinner.
5. The _____ light bulb needed to be changed.
6. Police work involves a lot of _____ when you're not busy.
7. The eagle was _____ that it was being watched with binoculars.
8. The hunters wanted to _____ the pesky raccoon.
9. The lion is definitely a _____.
10. It was _____ that the meal would cost so much.
11. It was _____ for it to be so hot in the winter.
12. Taylor acted as an _____ to the students.
13. Daniel received a _____ for his past crimes.
14. Yvette loved to grow tomatoes in her _____.
15. Honking the horn would surely _____ the deer.
16. Carla had a _____ about a giant spider as she slept.
17. The computer _____ helped us keep our accounting books.
18. Most people think newborn puppies are _____.

B. Copy the following sentence. **Anna put the old silverware and computer software into the storage unit that has a fluorescent light.**

_____

_____

_____

_____

Level 7, Lesson 20 – Words with **ar**, **are**, **or**, and **ore**

Date: _____

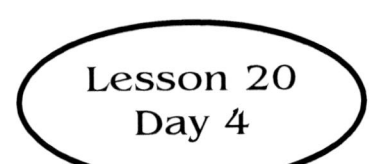

Lesson 20
Day 4

pardon	nightmare	abnormal	unforeseen
garden	silverware	advisor	carnivore
startle	software	adorable	boredom
sparkle	unaware	fedora	fluorescent
	ensnare	storage	

A. Underline the list word in each group that is spelled correctly.

1. storage — storege — storyage
2. florescent — fluorescent — floorescent
3. gardan — garden — gardin
4. silverwhare — silvewear — silverware
5. insnare — ensnare — ensnair
6. fadora — fedora — fedoora
7. boredom — boardom — boredum
8. unuware — unawere — unaware
9. abnormal — abnormel — abnorrmal
10. unforseen — unforeseen — unfourseen
11. nitemare — nightmaire — nightmare
12. pardon — pardun — pardone
13. advizer — advisor — advisur
14. carnivore — cornivore — carnivoore
15. adoorable — adorable — adoreable
16. softwhare — software — softwar
17. startle — startel — startil
18. sparkle — sparkel — sparkal

B. Write the definition from Day 1 for the list word **boredom**.

_____

_____

_____

Level 7, Lesson 20 – Words with **ar**, **are**, **or**, and **ore**

Date: _____

Lesson 20 - Day 5, Final Test

Correction Area:

1. _____
2. _____
3. _____
4. _____
5. _____
6. _____
7. _____
8. _____
9. _____
10. _____
11. _____
12. _____
13. _____
14. _____
15. _____
16. _____
17. _____
18. _____

Carry-over Words:

Correction Area:

1. _____
2. _____
3. _____
4. _____

Level 7, Lesson 20 – Words with **ar**, **are**, **or**, and **ore**

Date: _____

Words with **tch** and **sch**

1. **Review Your List Words**
   Look at the list words below and read each word to yourself. Then review each definition.

List Words/Definitions

homestretch *homestretch*	homeschool *homeschool*
• The last straight portion of a racetrack before crossing the finish line.	• Education that takes place in the home setting.
mismatch *mismatch*	**scholastic** *scholastic*
• An uneven or unfair matching of two opponents.	• Something that relates to school or education.
stopwatch *stopwatch*	**schooner** *schooner*
• A watch used to calculate the time from beginning to end of an event.	• A ship that has at least two masts.
topnotch *topnotch*	**schematic** *schematic*
• Something that is the best.	• A diagram of an electrical or mechanical system.
catchphrase *catchphrase*	**scholar** *scholar*
• A phrase that becomes popular.	• A person who is knowledgeable in one or more specific areas of study.
etching *etching*	**discharge** *discharge*
• Lines eaten into a surface by acid.	• The separation or release of something from another.
hatchery *hatchery*	**mischievous** *mischievous*
• A place where eggs are hatched.	• Playing in a naughty or teasing way.
hitchhiker *hitchhiker*	**scheme** *scheme*
• One who travels by getting free rides along a road.	• A formal plan that is sometimes carried out in secret.
ratchet *ratchet*	**schmooze** *schmooze*
• A type of device that is used to restrict motion in only one direction.	• To chat or talk in a friendly manner.

2. **Take Your Pretest**
   Turn to the next page to the Pretest section and your teacher will ask you to write each list word one at a time.

Level 7, Lesson 21 – Words with **tch** and **sch**

Date: _____

Pretest – Lesson 21: **Correction Area:**

1. _____ _____
2. _____ _____
3. _____ _____
4. _____ _____
5. _____ _____
6. _____ _____
7. _____ _____
8. _____ _____
9. _____ _____
10. _____ _____
11. _____ _____
12. _____ _____
13. _____ _____
14. _____ _____
15. _____ _____
16. _____ _____
17. _____ _____
18. _____ _____

Carry-over Words: **Correction Area:**

1. _____ _____
2. _____ _____
3. _____ _____
4. _____ _____

Level 7, Lesson 21 – Words with **tch** and **sch**

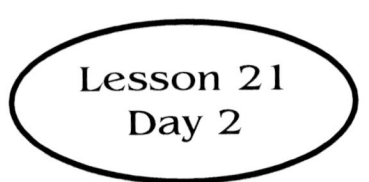

Lesson 21 Day 2

homestretch	catchphrase	homeschool	discharge
mismatch	etching	scholastic	mischievous
stopwatch	hatchery	schooner	scheme
topnotch	hitchhiker	schematic	schmooze
	ratchet	scholar	

A. Read each clue. Write the list word in the blanks that answers each clue. **Unscramble** the highlighted rows to find the answer to the question asked. Write the answer to the question in the spaces provided.

1. Times an event.
2. Chicks are everywhere.
3. Lines from acid.
4. Education related.
5. Carried out in secret.
6. Smart in an area.
7. Slightly bad conduct.

(Unscramble the letters above to find the answer.)

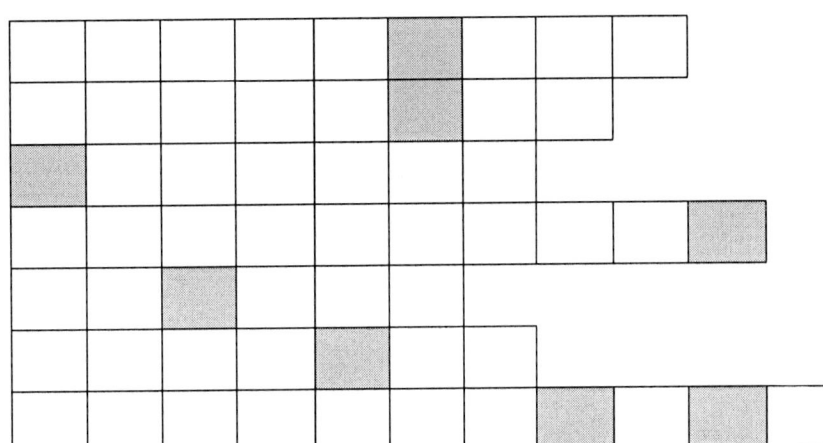

Mary definitely wanted to learn how to be a detective, but she was not sure how to get started. In other words, she did not _____.

Answer: "___ ___ ___ ___ **a** ___ ___ ___ ___"

B. Write the definition from Day 1 for the list word **ratchet**.

_____
_____
_____
_____

Level 7, Lesson 21 – Words with **tch** and **sch**

Date: _____

Lesson 21 Day 3

homestretch	catchphrase	homeschool	discharge
mismatch	etching	scholastic	mischievous
stopwatch	hatchery	schooner	scheme
topnotch	hitchhiker	schematic	schmooze
	ratchet	scholar	

A. Draw a line to connect each list word with its definition.

catchphrase	A watch used to calculate the time of an event.
etching	One who travels by getting free rides.
hatchery	A formal plan carried out in secret.
hitchhiker	Something that relates to school or education.
ratchet	A place where eggs are hatched.
homeschool	To chat or talk in a friendly manner.
scholastic	The separation or release of something.
schooner	A device that restricts motion to one direction.
schematic	Playing in a naughty or teasing way.
scholar	A diagram of an electrical or mechanical system.
homestretch	A person who is knowledgeable.
mismatch	Education that takes place in the home.
stopwatch	A phrase that becomes popular.
topnotch	Lines eaten into a surface by acid.
discharge	A ship that has two masts.
mischievous	Something that is the best.
scheme	An uneven or unfair matching of two opponents.
schmooze	The last straight portion before the finish line.

B. Copy the following sentence. **The hitchhiker was a scholar and wanted to schmooze with the driver of his ride.**

_____

_____

_____

Level 7, Lesson 21 – Words with **tch** and **sch**

Date: _____

Lesson 21 Day 4

homestretch	catchphrase	homeschool	discharge
mismatch	etching	scholastic	mischievous
stopwatch	hatchery	schooner	scheme
topnotch	hitchhiker	schematic	schmooze
	ratchet	scholar	

A. Write the list words that complete each sentence.

1. Jacob used a _____ to tighten the bolt.
2. The engineer needed the design _____ to build the computer.
3. Bradley was a _____ performer on the stage.
4. Kristin was a _____ in the area of oceanography.
5. The new employee wanted to laugh and _____ with her boss.
6. The horses raced down the _____ toward the finish line.
7. The coach used his _____ to time the runners.
8. The _____ turned out millions of chicks per year.
9. The _____ sailed around the world to its latest destination.
10. Grady was _____ and got into trouble at camp.
11. The new _____ became very popular in the advertisement.
12. Joe and Donald devised a _____ to win first prize.
13. We decided to _____ our children instead of sending them to school.
14. A game between short and tall basketball players is a _____.
15. The _____ on the glass spelled the business's name.
16. The boys had a _____ competition by answering trivia questions.
17. The _____ desperately needed a ride down the interstate.
18. The competitor was asked to _____ her weapon toward the target.

B. Write the definition from Day 1 for the list word **homestretch**.

_____

_____

_____

_____

Level 7, Lesson 21 – Words with **tch** and **sch**   125

Date: _____

Lesson 21 - Day 5, Final Test

Correction Area:

1. _____
2. _____
3. _____
4. _____
5. _____
6. _____
7. _____
8. _____
9. _____
10. _____
11. _____
12. _____
13. _____
14. _____
15. _____
16. _____
17. _____
18. _____

Carry-over Words:

Correction Area:

1. _____
2. _____
3. _____
4. _____

Level 7, Lesson 21 – Words with **tch** and **sch**

Date: _____

Lesson 22 Day 1

Words that begin with **bene**, **bon**, and **boun**

1. **Review Your List Words**
   Look at the list words below and read each word to yourself. Then review each definition.

List Words/Definitions

benefit *benefit*	bonkers *bonkers*
• Something that assists or helps a person.	• Someone who is mentally unstable.
benefactor *benefactor*	bond *bond*
• One who helps by giving money.	• A binding agreement.
beneficial *beneficial*	bongos *bongos*
• An act that results in being helpful.	• Two small drums attached to each other that are played with the fingers and hands.
beneficiary *beneficiary*	bound *bound*
• One who receives a benefit.	• Required by the law. Also to be tied and fastened.
benevolent *benevolent*	bounce *bounce*
• Kindness in giving. To be generous.	• A quick, springing jump into the air.
beneath *beneath*	bountiful *bountiful*
• A position which is lower than another position.	• Plentiful.
bonanza *bonanza*	boundary *boundary*
• An especially rich vein of precious ore. A source of great fortune or prosperity.	• A legally definable dividing line.
bonnet *bonnet*	bounty *bounty*
• A hat for a female that is tied under the chin by lace.	• Money given as an award for capturing a criminal.
bonfire *bonfire*	bonbon *bonbon*
• A large outdoor fire.	• A small chocolate covered piece of candy.

2. **Take Your Pretest**
   Turn to the next page to the Pretest section and your teacher will ask you to write each list word one at a time.

Level 7, Lesson 22 – Words Beginning with **bene**, **bon**, and **boun**

Date: _____

Pretest – Lesson 22:   **Correction Area:**

1. _____   _____
2. _____   _____
3. _____   _____
4. _____   _____
5. _____   _____
6. _____   _____
7. _____   _____
8. _____   _____
9. _____   _____
10. _____   _____
11. _____   _____
12. _____   _____
13. _____   _____
14. _____   _____
15. _____   _____
16. _____   _____
17. _____   _____
18. _____   _____

Carry-over Words: **Correction Area:**

1. _____   _____
2. _____   _____
3. _____   _____
4. _____   _____

Level 7, Lesson 22 – Words Beginning with **bene**, **bon**, and **boun**

Lesson 22 Day 2

Date: _____

benefit	benevolent	bonkers	bountiful
benefactor	beneath	bond	boundary
beneficial	bonanza	bongos	bounty
beneficiary	bonnet	bound	bonbon
	bonfire	bounce	

A. Find and circle each list word in the puzzle below.

```
T  O  N  B  H  Q  E  T  R  L  P  F  A  Q  H
B  N  T  X  V  M  X  J  O  D  V  L  H  Z  B
B  O  E  Q  X  M  Y  J  T  P  H  E  X  O  F
E  A  U  L  Y  R  A  I  C  I  F  E  N  E  B
N  D  Z  N  O  Y  Y  P  A  L  S  B  Q  S  A
E  Y  N  N  D  V  V  K  F  M  O  P  O  C  L
F  C  G  U  A  A  E  X  E  N  I  G  F  A  B
I  R  R  J  O  N  R  N  N  I  N  V  I  O  E
T  A  F  O  B  B  O  Y  E  O  N  C  N  B  R
H  H  T  A  E  N  E  B  B  B  I  K  D  O  I
B  O  U  N  T  I  F  U  L  F  E  P  N  N  F
B  O  U  N  T  Y  J  U  E  R  H  M  O  N  N
E  C  N  U  O  B  E  N  S  Z  X  G  B  E  O
L  Y  A  F  U  G  E  D  B  E  V  X  T  T  B
K  L  D  W  N  B  W  Y  I  R  Z  B  B  Y  F
```

B. Write the definition from Day 1 for the list word **bond**.

_____

_____

_____

_____

Level 7, Lesson 22 – Words Beginning with **bene**, **bon**, and **boun**

Date: _____

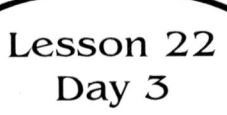

Lesson 22 Day 3

benefit	benevolent	bonkers	bountiful
benefactor	beneath	bond	boundary
beneficial	bonanza	bongos	bounty
beneficiary	bonnet	bound	bonbon
	bonfire	bounce	

A. Underline the list word in each group that is spelled correctly.

1. bonfire   bonfyre   bonfrie
2. bonet   bonnet   bonnit
3. bownce   bounce   bounse
4. bonbon   bonbone   bonnbon
5. bownty   bountie   bounty
6. boundary   boundery   boundrey
7. benefite   benefit   bennefit
8. bonkers   boncers   boncres
9. bennevolent benevolent   benevalent
10. bountiful   bouteful   bountaful
11. benefacter   benfactor   benefactor
12. benficial   beneficial   benefichal
13. benefishiary beneficiary   benneficairy
14. beneath   beneathe   beneeth
15. boneanza   bonanza   bonansa
16. bound   bounde   bouwnd
17. bonde   bondde   bond
18. bongos   bongoes   bonngos

B. Write a short paragraph below using at least four list words.

_____

_____

_____

_____

_____

Level 7, Lesson 22 – Words Beginning with **bene**, **bon**, and **boun**

Lesson 22 Day 4

Date: _____

benefit	benevolent	bonkers	bountiful
benefactor	beneath	bond	boundary
beneficial	bonanza	bongos	bounty
beneficiary	bonnet	bound	bonbon
	bonfire	bounce	

A. Use the following code to match the hint words.

A	B	C	D	E	F	G	H	I	J	K	L	M	N	O	P	Q	R	S	T	U	V	W	X	Y	Z
Ω	☺	⌘	❄	👎	😐	❆	☼	✎	📬	◆	◆	❀	⌘	❖	✈	◆	⊙	⏰	✪	⊞	✕	⧖	∞	☎	📖

1. Something that helps. _ _ _ _ _ _ _
2. Donates. _ _ _ _ _ _ _ _ _ _
3. Crazy. _ _ _ _ _ _ _
4. A binding agreement. _ _ _ _
5. Act was helpful. _ _ _ _ _ _ _ _ _ _
6. You tap them. _ _ _ _ _ _
7. Receives benefit. _ _ _ _ _ _ _ _ _ _ _
8. Fastened. _ _ _ _ _
9. Generous. _ _ _ _ _ _ _ _ _ _
10. To spring. _ _ _ _ _ _
11. Lower. _ _ _ _ _ _ _
12. More than enough. _ _ _ _ _ _ _ _ _
13. Precious ore. _ _ _ _ _ _ _
14. Line. _ _ _ _ _ _ _ _
15. Female cover. _ _ _ _ _ _
16. Reward. _ _ _ _ _ _
17. Outdoor fire. _ _ _ _ _ _ _
18. Chocolate. _ _ _ _ _ _

Level 7, Lesson 22 – Words Beginning with **bene**, **bon**, and **boun**

Date: _____

Lesson 22 - Day 5, Final Test

Correction Area:

1. _____
2. _____
3. _____
4. _____
5. _____
6. _____
7. _____
8. _____
9. _____
10. _____
11. _____
12. _____
13. _____
14. _____
15. _____
16. _____
17. _____
18. _____

Carry-over Words:

Correction Area:

1. _____
2. _____
3. _____
4. _____

Level 7, Lesson 22 – Words Beginning with **bene**, **bon**, and **boun**

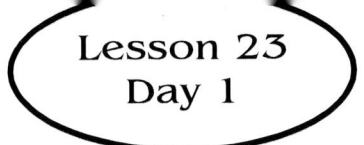

Words with consonant blends cl and cr

Date: _____

1. Review Your List Words
Look at the list words below and read each word to yourself. Then review each definition.

List Words/Definitions

clarification *clarification* • To make something more easily understood.	**created** *created* • Something that was made or invented.
classical *classical* • Concerns the general studies of arts and sciences.	**craftsman** *craftsman* • One who possesses great skill in a particular craft.
classified *classified* • To be placed in a specific group or class.	**credential** *credential* • A document attesting to the truth of certain stated facts.
cleanliness *cleanliness* • The condition of being clean.	**credulous** *credulous* • Quick to believe something not supported by fact. Gullible.
clearance *clearance* • The amount of space between two objects before they collide. Also, the process of clearing.	**croissant** *croissant* • A flaky roll shaped like a crescent.
clemency *clemency* • Mercy or leniency.	**crossroad** *crossroad* • A smaller road that crosses a main road.
clothing *clothing* • Garments that are worn by humans.	**crucible** *crucible* • A pot not easily damaged by fire. Made for melting metal.
clumsy *clumsy* • To move in an awkward or ungraceful manner.	**democracy** *democracy* • A government selected by the people and run by majority rule.
conclusion *conclusion* • The ending of something.	**increase** *increase* • To make greater.

2. Take Your Pretest
Turn to the next page to the Pretest section and your teacher will ask you to write each list word one at a time.

Date: _____

Pretest – Lesson 23:   Correction Area:

1. _____   _____
2. _____   _____
3. _____   _____
4. _____   _____
5. _____   _____
6. _____   _____
7. _____   _____
8. _____   _____
9. _____   _____
10. _____   _____
11. _____   _____
12. _____   _____
13. _____   _____
14. _____   _____
15. _____   _____
16. _____   _____
17. _____   _____
18. _____   _____

Carry-over Words: Correction Area:

1. _____   _____
2. _____   _____
3. _____   _____
4. _____   _____

Level 7, Lesson 23 – Words with consonant blends **cl** and **cr**

Date: _____

clarification	clearance	created	crossroad
classical	clemency	craftsman	crucible
classified	clothing	credential	democracy
cleanliness	clumsy	credulous	increase
	conclusion	croissant	

A. Cross out the word that is spelled incorrectly. Write the correctly spelled words on the lines.

1. (conclusion, conclusian) _____
2. (crossant, croissant) _____
3. (increase, increese) _____
4. (clarafication, clarification) _____
5. (clearence, clearance) _____
6. (created, creatid) _____
7. (cricable, crucible) _____
8. (democracy, demokracy) _____
9. (cleanliness, cleanlness) _____
10. (classical, classicle) _____
11. (classified, classifed) _____
12. (craftsman, craftman) _____
13. (credential, credental) _____
14. (crossroad, crossrode) _____
15. (clemancy, clemency) _____
16. (clothing, cloething) _____
17. (credulous, credulis) _____
18. (clumbsey, clumsy) _____

B. Write two sentences below using at least two list words in each sentence.

_____
_____
_____
_____

Level 7, Lesson 23 – Words with consonant blends **cl** and **cr**

Lesson 23 Day 3

Date: _____

clarification	clearance	created	crossroad
classical	clemency	craftsman	crucible
classified	clothing	credential	democracy
cleanliness	clumsy	credulous	increase
	conclusion	croissant	

A. Unscramble the following list words.

calriifcoatin

1. _____

celraance

2. _____

cconluison

3. _____

irnceeas

4. _____

dceamorcy

5. _____

corsrsoad

6. _____

calsiscal

7. _____

culmsy

8. _____

colhting

9. _____

cdreetnial

10. _____

ceraetd

11. _____

cfratsamn

12. _____

curicble

13. _____

coriassnt

14. _____

curedolus

15. _____

celmnecy

16. _____

calsisfied

17. _____

calenilness

18. _____

B. Write the definition from Day 1 for the list word **crucible**.

_____

_____

_____

_____

Level 7, Lesson 23 – Words with consonant blends **cl** and **cr**

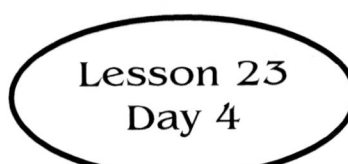

Date: _____

clarification	clearance	created	crossroad
classical	clemency	craftsman	crucible
classified	clothing	credential	democracy
cleanliness	clumsy	credulous	increase
	conclusion	croissant	

A. Draw a line to connect each list word with its definition.

crossroad   A government selected and run by the people.

created   To make greater.

clearance   Mercy or leniency.

clarification   To move in an awkward or ungraceful manner.

classical   The ending of something.

clemency   A pot not easily damaged by fire.

craftsman   A smaller road that crosses a main road.

crucible   Garments worn by humans.

democracy   A flaky roll shaped like a crescent.

credential   Quick to believe something not supported by fact.

clothing   The space between two objects.

classified   The condition of being clean.

cleanliness   A document attesting to the truth of certain facts.

clumsy   To be placed in a specific group or class.

credulous   One who possesses great skill in a particular craft.

increase   Concerns the general studies.

conclusion   Something that was made or invented.

croissant   To make something more easily understood.

Level 7, Lesson 23 – Words with consonant blends **cl** and **cr**   137

Date: _____

Lesson 23 - Day 5, Final Test

Correction Area:

1. _____
2. _____
3. _____
4. _____
5. _____
6. _____
7. _____
8. _____
9. _____
10. _____
11. _____
12. _____
13. _____
14. _____
15. _____
16. _____
17. _____
18. _____

Carry-over Words:

Correction Area:

1. _____
2. _____
3. _____
4. _____

Level 7, Lesson 23 – Words with consonant blends **cl** and **cr**

Lesson 24 Review Day 1

Review of words that have to do with feelings or emotions

List Words

beautiful	complacent	frightened	sleepy
patient	ecstatic	confident	rested
disgusted	hopeful	distracted	compassionate
infuriated	exhausted	helplessness	enthusiastic
	apprehensive	depressed	

A. Write each group of three list words in alphabetical order.

confident, complacent, depressed

1. _____ 2. _____ 3. _____

helplessness, hopeful, disgusted

4. _____ 5. _____ 6. _____

rested, patient, frightened

7. _____ 8. _____ 9. _____

sleepy, distracted, exhausted

10. _____ 11. _____ 12. _____

apprehensive, enthusiastic, compassionate

13. _____ 14. _____ 15. _____

ecstatic, beautiful, infuriated

16. _____ 17. _____ 18. _____

complacent, distracted, exhausted

19. _____ 20. _____ 21. _____

rested, exhausted, infuriated

22. _____ 23. _____ 24. _____

enthusiastic, patient, confident

25. _____ 26. _____ 27. _____

Level 7, Lesson 24, Review of lessons 19-23

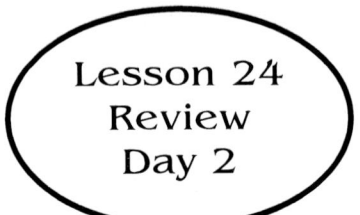

Review of words with ar, are, or, and ore

List Words

pardon	nightmare	abnormal	unforeseen
garden	silverware	advisor	carnivore
startle	software	adorable	boredom
sparkle	unaware	fedora	fluorescent
	ensnare	storage	

A. Read each clue. Write the list word in the blanks that answers each clue. **Unscramble** the highlighted rows to find the answer to the question asked. Write the answer to the question in the spaces provided.

1. A scary dream.
2. To frighten.
3. Fork, spoon, knife.
4. To capture or trap.
5. Cute.
6. A felt hat with a brim.
7. Extra space.
8. Feeds upon meat.
9. A light bulb.

(Unscramble the letters above to find the answer.)

When Susan had a chance to become a lifeguard at the local pool, she loved the idea. You could say that she _____.

Answer: "__ __ __ __   __ __ __ __ __ __ __ __ __ __   __in__"

Level 7, Lesson 24, Review of lessons 19-23

Lesson 24 Review Day 3

Review of words with **tch** and **sch**

List Words

homestretch	catchphrase	homeschool	discharge
mismatch	etching	scholastic	mischievous
stopwatch	hatchery	schooner	scheme
topnotch	hitchhiker	schematic	schmooze
	ratchet	scholar	

A. Find and circle each list word in the puzzle below.

```
H J C L S E E R N E H M O H R
C O I I S C A T G A I R A M E
A E M X T T H R C S Y T D I K
T E V E C S A E C H C I P S I
C G M H S H A H M H I F D M H
H M E E C T I L E A D N D A H
P T V S H E R R O L T O G T C
H L I M V C Y E S H Y I H C T
R D V O B G S X T L C S C H I
A Z U R E N O O H C S S T X H
S S T O P W A T C H H E O S R
E Z V S C H M O O Z E L N U A
R A L O H C S T P S E R P V G
K V H H I F W R P C L R O A A
L O O H C S E M O H E A T K U
```

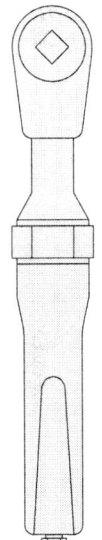

Level 7, Lesson 24, Review of lessons 19-23

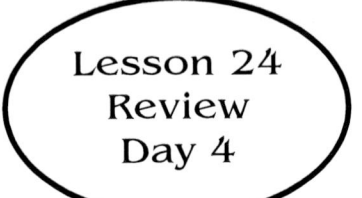

Lesson 24 Review Day 4

Review of words that begin with bene, bon, and boun

List Words

benefit	benevolent	bonkers	bountiful
benefactor	beneath	bond	boundary
beneficial	bonanza	bongos	bounty
beneficiary	bonnet	bound	bonbon
	bonfire	bounce	

A. Underline the list word in each sentence that is spelled incorrectly.

1. The advantage of the bonefire was that everyone stayed warm.
2. It was benefical to have the firefighters standing by whenever dad cooked.
3. The millionaire was extremely benevalent when it came time to donate.
4. The children loved to bownce on the inflatable structure.
5. Kelli and I stayed home and shared a bohnbon.
6. His wife was the only beneficary of his last will and testament.
7. Carol was bounde by the terms and conditions of her legal contract.
8. The fall harvest provided a bountifull amount of food for us.
9. The school was a benefacter of grant money from the state.
10. The sound of the roaring crowd made Karen go boncers for a bit.
11. There was a boundarie line between the two houses.
12. There is a bennefit to having a friend who is in congress.
13. The treasure was buried beanethe the porch of her house.
14. The miners hit a bonansza in the mine and were finally able to retire early.
15. The baby wore a frilly bonet.
16. The bonde issued by the State of California paid eight percent interest.
17. Milton broke out the bongeos and was the main attraction at the get together.
18. Cindy and Theresa collected a bountey for returning the lost kitten.

B. Correctly write the list words from above in order.

1. _____ 2. _____
3. _____ 4. _____
5. _____ 6. _____
7. _____ 8. _____
9. _____ 10. _____
11. _____ 12. _____
13. _____ 14. _____
15. _____ 16. _____
17. _____ 18. _____

Level 7, Lesson 24, Review of lessons 19-23

Lesson 24 Review Day 5

Review of words with consonant blends cl and cr

Date: _____

List Words

clarification	clearance	created	crossroad
classical	clemency	craftsman	crucible
classified	clothing	credential	democracy
cleanliness	clumsy	credulous	increase
	conclusion	croissant	

A. Finish the crossword puzzle.

Across:
7. To make or invent.
9. To make more understandable.
12. The end of something.
13. You can melt metal in it.
14. To move in an awkward fashion.
15. Garments worn by humans.
16. Leniency or forgiveness.
17. General study of arts and science.

Down:
1. A distance between two parts.
2. A road that crosses another.
3. To be placed in a specific class.
4. One skilled in a craft.
5. To believe without facts.
6. A document attesting to truth about facts.
8. A government elected and ran by the people.
9. A crescent-shaped, flaky roll.
10. The act of being clean.
11. To make greater.

Level 7, Lesson 24, Review of lessons 19-23

<<This page intentionally left blank>>

Lesson 25 Day 1

Words with silent letters

1. **Review Your List Words**
Look at the list words below and read each word to yourself. Then review each definition.

Notice that each word below has a **silent letter** or **silent letter pair**, meaning that it is not pronounced when the word is spoken. The silent letters in each word have been underlined for you.

List Words/Definitions

plum<u>b</u>er *plumber*	One who works on systems that supply or remove water or waste from structures.	sole<u>mn</u> *solemn*	To be very serious or formal.
ras<u>p</u>berry *raspberry*	A sweet black or red berry that is edible.	len<u>g</u>th *length*	The distance between the farthest ends of an item.
kno<u>w</u>ledge *knowledge*	Skill gained by experience.	<u>w</u>ritten *written*	Words put down on paper.
<u>k</u>ni<u>gh</u>t *knight*	A warrior who served a king and fought rivals on horseback.	spa<u>gh</u>etti *spaghetti*	Long, stringy pasta noodles.
campai<u>gn</u> *campaign*	A series of events designed to win an elected position.	hei<u>gh</u>t *height*	The maximum upward distance of an object from a lower point.
han<u>d</u>some *handsome*	A term for a male who is pleasing in appearance.	dou<u>gh</u>nut *doughnut*	A sweet, round pastry with a hole in the middle.
gourme<u>t</u> *gourmet*	A person who enjoys and knows a lot about food and drink.	condem<u>n</u> *condemn*	To declare to be unfit for use.
han<u>d</u>kerchie<u>f</u> *handkerchief*	A small piece of cloth used to wipe the face or nose.	<u>w</u>reckage *wreckage*	Damaged items that remain after a destructive event.
r<u>h</u>ythm *rhythm*	A steady, consistent beat.	cons<u>c</u>ious *conscious*	To be mentally aware or active.

2. **Take Your Pretest**
Turn to the next page to the Pretest section and your teacher will ask you to write each list word one at a time.

Level 7, Lesson 25 – Words with silent letters

Date: _____

Pretest – Lesson 25: **Correction Area:**

1. _____ _____
2. _____ _____
3. _____ _____
4. _____ _____
5. _____ _____
6. _____ _____
7. _____ _____
8. _____ _____
9. _____ _____
10. _____ _____
11. _____ _____
12. _____ _____
13. _____ _____
14. _____ _____
15. _____ _____
16. _____ _____
17. _____ _____
18. _____ _____

Carry-over Words: **Correction Area:**

1. _____ _____
2. _____ _____
3. _____ _____
4. _____ _____

Level 7, Lesson 25 – Words with silent letters

Date: _____

Lesson 25
Day 2

plumber	campaign	solemn	doughnut
raspberry	handsome	length	condemn
knowledge	gourmet	written	wreckage
knight	handkerchief	spaghetti	conscious
	rhythm	height	

A. Use the misspelled words below as a guide to find and write the properly spelled list words. Pay special attention to the silent letters in each word.

rasberry

1. _____

rythm

2. _____

heit

3. _____

consious

4. _____

campain

5. _____

solem

6. _____

dounut

7. _____

reckage

8. _____

condem

9. _____

hansome

10. _____

gourme

11. _____

lenth

12. _____

ritten

13. _____

plumer

14. _____

spagetti

15. _____

hankerchief

16. _____

nit

17. _____

nowledge

18. _____

B. Write the definition from Day 1 for the list word **doughnut**.

_____

_____

_____

Level 7, Lesson 25 – Words with silent letters

Lesson 25 Day 3

Date: _____

plumber	campaign	solemn	doughnut
raspberry	handsome	length	condemn
knowledge	gourmet	written	wreckage
knight	handkerchief	spaghetti	conscious
	rhythm	height	

A. **Proofreading.** Underline any words that are misspelled. Insert **punctuation** where needed. Mark an **X** through any letters that are incorrectly **capitalized** or through any incorrect **punctuation**. Circle any letters that should be **capitalized** but are not. Correctly write the list words in the order they appear in the below paragraphs.

while the gormay ate spagettti! the hansome politician with noledge had ritten a solem speech for his campain to condem old Unseaworthy ships   in his, speech he spoke of a plummer and an english nite who had survived the, ship's reckage. a lenth of that kept them above the Water by a hite of only one inch? They remained consious throughout the ordeal by sharing a razberry donut, waiving a hanjerchiff, and by singing old survival songs in perfect rithym?

B. Correctly write the list words in the order they appear in the above paragraph.

1. _____ 2. _____ 3. _____
4. _____ 5. _____ 6. _____
7. _____ 8. _____ 9. _____
10. _____ 11. _____ 12. _____
13. _____ 14. _____ 15. _____
16. _____ 17. _____ 18. _____

C. Write the list words that match the dictionary pronunciations.

1. ˈplŭm-ər _____
2. ˈrĕk-ĭj _____
3. ˈrĭt-n _____
4. spə-ˈgĕt-ē _____
5. ˈsŏl-əm _____
6. ˈdō-nət _____
7. ˈhăn-səm _____
8. ˈnīt _____
9. ˈrĭth-əm _____

10. ˈrăz-ˌbĕr-ē _____
11. kăm-ˈpān _____
12. kən-ˈdĕm _____
13. ˈkŏn-shəs _____
14. ˈlĕnkth _____
15. ˈhăng-kər-chĭf _____
16. ˈnŏl-ĭj _____
17. ˈgu̇r-ˌmā _____
18. hīt _____

Level 7, Lesson 25 – Words with silent letters

Lesson 25 Day 4

plumber	campaign	solemn	doughnut
raspberry	handsome	length	condemn
knowledge	gourmet	written	wreckage
knight	handkerchief	spaghetti	conscious
	rhythm	height	

A. Underline the word in parentheses that makes sense to complete the sentence. Write the correctly spelled words on the lines below

1. The (plummer, plumber) fixed our leaky faucet.
2. The (nite, knight) jousted other combatants in the contest.
3. Darren keeps perfect (rythym, rhythm) while playing the bongo drums.
4. The poem was (ritten, written) on a blue piece of paper.
5. After waking up from her nap, Beth was (contious, conscious) and alert.
6. The (reckage, wreckage) from the accident was scattered everywhere.
7. After viewing the old barn, the city decided to (condemn, condem) and tear it down.
8. Everyone in our family loves a delicious (doughnut, dounut) for breakfast.
9. Evan possessed great (knowledge, nowledge) of government and politics.
10. Mike and Katie loved to eat each (razberry, raspberry) one at a time.
11. Verna used a (handkerchief, hankerchiff) to wipe her brow.
12. Kristin and her father love to make homemade (spagetti, spaghetti) and bread.
13. The horse reached a (height, heite) that was equal to my tall brother.
14. Corey wore a (lenth, length) of rope around his waist as a belt.
15. The senator started his (campane, campaign) to be re-elected.
16. Will was chosen as the most (handsome, hansome) boy in the contest.
17. Aunt Jessie had prepared a delicious (gormay, gourmet) meal for us.
18. Darrel's commencement speech was a (solemn, solem) event.

1. _____ 2. _____
3. _____ 4. _____
5. _____ 6. _____
7. _____ 8. _____
9. _____ 10. _____
11. _____ 12. _____
13. _____ 14. _____
15. _____ 16. _____
17. _____ 18. _____

B. Write the definition from Day 1 for the list word **conscious**.

_____

_____

Level 7, Lesson 25 – Words with silent letters

Date: _____

Lesson 25 - Day 5, Final Test

Correction Area:

1. _____
2. _____
3. _____
4. _____
5. _____
6. _____
7. _____
8. _____
9. _____
10. _____
11. _____
12. _____
13. _____
14. _____
15. _____
16. _____
17. _____
18. _____

Carry-over Words:

Correction Area:

1. _____
2. _____
3. _____
4. _____

Level 7, Lesson 25 – Words with silent letters

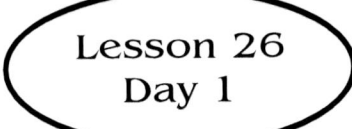

Easily misspelled words

Date: _____

1. **Review Your List Words**
   Look at the list words below and read each word to yourself. Then review each definition.

List Words/Definitions

changeable *changeable* • Something that can be amended or changed.		**minuscule** *minuscule* • Something that is very small, even smaller than a miniature.	
discipline *discipline* • Habit or traits that are followed by practice.		**perseverance** *perseverance* • Not giving up even though challenges are present.	
exhilarate *exhilarate* • To make something exciting.		**possession** *possession* • The act of owning something.	
guarantee *guarantee* • Assurance that something is as promised.		**questionnaire** *questionnaire* • A list of questions asked to obtain information or opinions.	
hierarchy *hierarchy* • Different layers or levels of importance.		**supersede** *supersede* • To take the place or position of another.	
inoculate *inoculate* • An injection of medicine into a living thing to protect or treat a disease.		**vacuum** *vacuum* • The absence of air within a space.	
maneuver *maneuver* • To steer or guide carefully.		**definitely** *definitely* • Unquestionable. No room for doubt.	
medieval *medieval* • Something that is related to the Middle Ages of mankind.		**congratulations** *congratulations* • The expression of happiness for another's success.	
miniature *miniature* • A smaller version or copy of something.		**liaison** *liaison* • A go-between or representative who mediates.	

2. **Take Your Pretest**
   Turn to the next page to the Pretest section and your teacher will ask you to write each list word one at a time.

Date: _____

Pretest – Lesson 26: **Correction Area:**

1. _____ _____
2. _____ _____
3. _____ _____
4. _____ _____
5. _____ _____
6. _____ _____
7. _____ _____
8. _____ _____
9. _____ _____
10. _____ _____
11. _____ _____
12. _____ _____
13. _____ _____
14. _____ _____
15. _____ _____
16. _____ _____
17. _____ _____
18. _____ _____

Carry-over Words: **Correction Area:**

1. _____ _____
2. _____ _____
3. _____ _____
4. _____ _____

Level 7, Lesson 26 – Easily misspelled words

Lesson 26 Day 2

Date: _____

changeable	hierarchy	minuscule	vacuum
discipline	inoculate	perseverance	definitely
exhilarate	maneuver	possession	congratulations
guarantee	medieval	questionnaire	liaison
	miniature	supersede	

A. Find and circle each list word in the puzzle below.

```
E  S  Y  L  E  T  I  N  I  F  E  D  A  E  E
T  N  P  O  S  S  E  S  S  I  O  N  H  R  I
A  O  G  U  A  R  A  N  T  E  E  D  I  U  S
R  I  V  M  C  M  E  D  I  E  V  A  L  T  D
A  T  A  A  C  H  T  P  M  N  N  J  M  A  I
L  A  C  N  V  M  A  P  A  N  C  M  L  I  S
I  L  U  E  L  I  H  N  O  B  D  D  Q  N  C
H  U  U  G  N  P  I  G  S  H  H  T  I  I
X  T  M  V  U  U  T  U  E  E  V  D  Z  M  P
E  A  P  E  R  S  E  V  E  R  A  N  C  E  L
H  R  J  R  E  C  R  Y  V  L  A  B  N  N  I
E  G  R  U  J  U  X  N  I  U  Q  R  L  M  N
E  N  Q  C  F  L  I  A  I  S  O  N  C  E  E
Q  O  S  U  P  E  R  S  E  D  E  N  D  H  I
W  C  G  P  G  E  T  A  L  U  C  O  N  I  Y
```

B. Write the definition from Day 1 for the list word **questionnaire**.

_____

_____

_____

Level 7, Lesson 26 – Easily misspelled words

Lesson 26
Day 3

changeable	hierarchy	minuscule	vacuum
discipline	inoculate	perseverance	definitely
exhilarate	maneuver	possession	congratulations
guarantee	medieval	questionnaire	liaison
	miniature	supersede	

A. Finish each list word.

1. _____era_____
2. i_____cu_____
3. _____ve_____
4. _____fi_____
5. ____an_____
6. ____os_____
7. ch_____
8. ____is_____
9. ____x_____
10. _____nn_____
11. _____ai_____
12. _____gr_____
13. _____an_____
14. _____uu_____
15. _____tur_____
16. ____ed_____
17. _____pe_____
18. _____nu_____

B. Write a short paragraph below using at least five list words.

_____
_____
_____
_____
_____
_____
_____
_____
_____

Level 7, Lesson 26 – Easily misspelled words

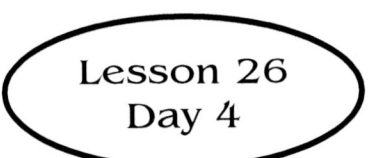

Lesson 26 Day 4

changeable	hierarchy	minuscule	vacuum
discipline	inoculate	perseverance	definitely
exhilarate	maneuver	possession	congratulations
guarantee	medieval	questionnaire	liaison
	miniature	supersede	

A. Write each group of three list words in alphabetical order.

possession, perseverance, liaison

1. _____ 2. _____ 3. _____

miniature, medieval, maneuver

4. _____ 5. _____ 6. _____

definitely, changeable, discipline

7. _____ 8. _____ 9. _____

hierarchy, inoculate, guarantee

10. _____ 11. _____ 12. _____

minuscule, medieval, miniature

13. _____ 14. _____ 15. _____

questionnaire, vacuum, exhilarate

16. _____ 17. _____ 18. _____

supersede, congratulations, changeable

19. _____ 20. _____ 21. _____

supersede, liaison, miniature

22. _____ 23. _____ 24. _____

hierarchy, exhilarate, definitely

25. _____ 26. _____ 27. _____

congratulations, changeable, inoculate

28. _____ 29. _____ 30. _____

Level 7, Lesson 26 – Easily misspelled words

Date: _____

Lesson 26 - Day 5, Final Test

Correction Area:

1. _____   _____
2. _____   _____
3. _____   _____
4. _____   _____
5. _____   _____
6. _____   _____
7. _____   _____
8. _____   _____
9. _____   _____
10. _____   _____
11. _____   _____
12. _____   _____
13. _____   _____
14. _____   _____
15. _____   _____
16. _____   _____
17. _____   _____
18. _____   _____

Carry-over Words: Correction Area:

1. _____   _____
2. _____   _____
3. _____   _____
4. _____   _____

Level 7, Lesson 26 – Easily misspelled words

Lesson 27 Day 1

Words with different s sounds

1. **Review Your List Word**
   Look at the list words below and read each word to yourself. Then review each definition.

   The letter **s** makes many different sounds depending on the word.

   -The **s** in the word **consider** makes the **s** sound.

   -The **s** in **usable** makes a **z** sound.

   -The **s** in the word **measure** makes the **zh** sound.

List Words/Definitions

consider *consider*	accuse *accuse*
• To take some time to make a decision about something.	• To place blame or allege misconduct or wrongdoing.
disaster *disaster*	residual *residual*
• A sudden event that causes a lot of damage.	• The portion that remains after the main portion is taken away.
satisfy *satisfy*	desire *desire*
• To appease or make content.	• To crave or wish for something.
surrender *surrender*	measure *measure*
• To yield or give up to something.	• To find the size of something by using a device such as a ruler.
simple *simple*	pleasure *pleasure*
• To be very modest or easy.	• A feeling of excitement or joy.
insulate *insulate*	usual *usual*
• To shelter or shield from something.	• Something that is normal or commonplace.
usable *usable*	foreclosure *foreclosure*
• Something that is in a condition that can be used.	• A legal procedure where the lender takes back the collateral for non-payment of a loan.
positive *positive*	visual *visual*
• To be certain or confident of something.	• Something that can be seen with eyes.
poison *poison*	casual *casual*
• A substance formulated to injure or kill a plant or animal.	• Relaxed or informal.

2. **Take Your Pretest**
   Turn to the next page to the Pretest section and your teacher will ask you to write each list word one at a time.

Date: _____

Pretest – Lesson 27:

1. _____
2. _____
3. _____
4. _____
5. _____
6. _____
7. _____
8. _____
9. _____
10. _____
11. _____
12. _____
13. _____
14. _____
15. _____
16. _____
17. _____
18. _____

Correction Area:

_____
_____
_____
_____
_____
_____
_____
_____
_____
_____
_____
_____
_____
_____
_____
_____
_____
_____

Carry-over Words:

1. _____
2. _____
3. _____
4. _____

Correction Area:

_____
_____
_____
_____

Level 7, Lesson 27- Words with different **s** sounds

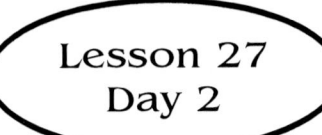

Lesson 27 Day 2

consider	simple	accuse	usual
disaster	insulate	residual	foreclosure
satisfy	usable	desire	visual
surrender	positive	measure	casual
	poison	pleasure	

Date: _____

A. Write the list words that complete each sentence.

1. The army lost the battle and had to _____.
2. The farmer bought some _____ to get rid of pests.
3. Going for a ride in the new car brought him much _____.
4. The bank initiated _____ proceedings on the unpaid loan.
5. The official had to _____ the distance of the pole vault.
6. We had to seriously _____ Bob's offer to purchase the used car.
7. The wool gloves would _____ her hands from the cold.
8. The painting was very plain and _____ with only straight lines.
9. They had a strong _____ to move to another house.
10. The _____ medicine left in the bottle was not enough for a dose.
11. The victim did _____ the man of trying to steal her purse.
12. Tony would say all of the _____ things he always says.
13. His _____ inspection of the car was that it was indeed blue.
14. The meeting was supposed to be relaxed and _____.
15. Gary can _____ his hunger by eating a candy bar.
16. The left over grass fertilizer in the bottle was still _____.
17. Alice was _____ that she did not want to wash Dan's dirty car.
18. The tornado was a _____ as it tore through the town.

B. Write the definition from Day 1 for the list word **usual**.

_____

_____

_____

_____

Level 7, Lesson 27- Words with different **s** sounds

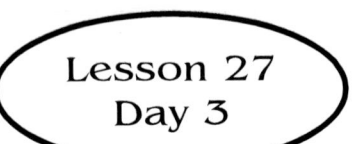

Lesson 27 Day 3

Date: _____

consider	simple	accuse	usual
disaster	insulate	residual	foreclosure
satisfy	usable	desire	visual
surrender	positive	measure	casual
	poison	pleasure	

A. Write a list word that matches each definition.

1. Something that can be used.

2. Relaxed or informal.

3. To shelter or shield from something.

4. The portion that remains.

5. Something that can be seen.

6. To place blame or allege misconduct.

7. To yield or give up to something.

8. To be certain or confident.

9. A feeling of excitement or joy.

10. Take some time to decide.

11. To be very modest or easy.

12. A substance formulated to injure or kill.

13. To appease or make content.

14. A legal procedure for an unpaid loan.

15. To crave or wish for something.

16. Something that is normal.

17. A sudden event that causes damage.

18. To find the size of something.

B. Copy the following sentence. **The decorator did a simple design in the living room to satisfy her usual client.**

_____

_____

_____

Level 7, Lesson 27- Words with different **s** sounds

Date: _____

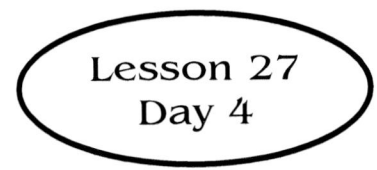

Lesson 27
Day 4

consider	simple	accuse	usual
disaster	insulate	residual	foreclosure
satisfy	usable	desire	visual
surrender	positive	measure	casual
	poison	pleasure	

A. Use the following code to finish the sentences.

A	B	C	D	E	F	G	H	I	J	K	L	M	N	O	P	Q	R	S	T	U	V	W	X	Y	Z
Ω	☺	✊	❄	☝	☹	❆	☼	✎	📷	◇	◆	⚽	⌘	❖	✈	●	☉	⏱	✪	⊕	✕	⌛	✍	☎	📖

1. The non-stop rain caused quite a ___ ___ ___ ___ ___ ___ ___ ___.
    ❄ ✎ ⏱ Ω ⏱ ✪ ☹ ☉

2. The hat would ___ ___ ___ ___ ___ ___ ___ ___ Jared's head from the cold.
    ✎ ⌘ ⏱ ⊕ ◆ Ω ✪ ☹

3. Jan would have to ___ ___ ___ ___ ___ ___ ___ the amount of milk in the glass.
    ⚽ ☹ Ω ⏱ ⊕ ☉ ☹

4. The ___ ___ ___ ___ ___ ___ impact of the painting was undeniable.
    ✕ ✎ ⏱ ⊕ Ω ◆

5. The ___ ___ ___ ___ ___ ___ was not strong enough to have any effect.
    ✈ ❖ ✎ ⏱ ❖ ⌘

6. It was a ___ ___ ___ ___ ___ ___ ___ ___ finally to meet the president.
    ✈ ◆ ☹ Ω ⏱ ⊕ ☉ ☹

7. Friday was always ___ ___ ___ ___ ___ ___ day at work; we could wear jeans.
    ✊ Ω ⏱ ⊕ Ω ◆

8. The bank started a ___ ___ ___ ___ ___ ___ ___ ___ ___ ___ on their part.
    ☺ ❖ ☉ ☹ ✊ ◆ ❖ ⏱ ⊕ ☉ ☹

9. The ___ ___ ___ ___ ___ ___ ___ ___ crumbs in the cookie jar were still delicious.
    ☉ ☹ ⏱ ✎ ❄ ⊕ Ω ◆

10. Mom would ___ ___ ___ ___ ___ ___ Tommy of snooping for presents.
    Ω ✊ ✊ ⊕ ⏱ ☹

11. The answer to the question was ___ ___ ___ ___ ___ ___.
    ⏱ ✎ ❄ ✈ ◆ ☹

12. It was ___ ___ ___ ___ ___ for us to eat lunch at noon.
    ⊕ ⏱ ⊕ Ω ◆

13. The old table with a broken leg is still ___ ___ ___ ___ ___ ___.
    ⊕ ⏱ Ω ☺ ◆ ☹

14. It was her ___ ___ ___ ___ ___ ___ to own a pony.
    ❄ ☹ ⏱ ✎ ☉ ☹

15. Lisa could ___ ___ ___ ___ ___ ___ ___ her hunger by eating breakfast.
    ⏱ Ω ✪ ✎ ⏱ ☺ ☎

16. Debbie was ___ ___ ___ ___ ___ ___ ___ that she had never eaten eel before.
    ✈ ❖ ⏱ ✎ ✪ ✎ ✕ ☹

17. The green team would have to ___ ___ ___ ___ ___ ___ ___ ___ ___ to the red team.
    ⏱ ⊕ ❖ ☉ ☹ ⌘ ❄ ☹ ☉

18. Her boss said he would ___ ___ ___ ___ ___ ___ ___ ___ giving Melba a raise.
    ✊ ❖ ⌘ ⏱ ✎ ❄ ☹ ☉

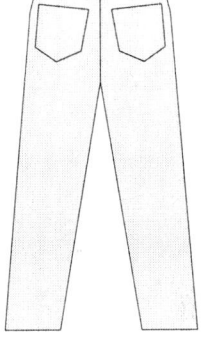

Level 7, Lesson 27- Words with different **s** sounds

161

Date: _____

Lesson 27 - Day 5, Final Test

Correction Area:

1. _____ _____
2. _____ _____
3. _____ _____
4. _____ _____
5. _____ _____
6. _____ _____
7. _____ _____
8. _____ _____
9. _____ _____
10. _____ _____
11. _____ _____
12. _____ _____
13. _____ _____
14. _____ _____
15. _____ _____
16. _____ _____
17. _____ _____
18. _____ _____

Carry-over Words: Correction Area:

1. _____ _____
2. _____ _____
3. _____ _____
4. _____ _____

Level 7, Lesson 27- Words with different **s** sounds

Date: _____

Lesson 28 Day 1

Words with **over** and **out**

1. **Review Your List Words**
   Look at the list words below and read each word to yourself. Then review each definition.

List Words/Definitions

carryover *carryover*	bailout *bailout*
• Something brought forward from an earlier time or period.	• To rescue from financial difficulties.
discovered *discovered*	cookout *cookout*
• Something found for the first time.	• To prepare food outdoors with a flame.
governor *governor*	devout *devout*
• The head of a state government.	• Someone who is devoted to religion.
controversy *controversy*	outrageous *outrageous*
• A quarrel or disagreement.	• Something that is extremely inappropriate or indecent.
leftover *leftover*	outburst *outburst*
• Food remaining from a meal.	• A sudden blurting or loud noise from a human.
overrated *overrated*	outcome *outcome*
• To place a value on something that is too high.	• The result of something.
overcoat *overcoat*	checkout *checkout*
• A sturdy garment worn over regular clothing to keep warm.	• The process of paying for goods to be purchased.
recovery *recovery*	outgoing *outgoing*
• To regain normal heath. Also to regain something lost or taken.	• Someone who is friendly and sociable to others.
takeover *takeover*	outdated *outdated*
• To assume or take control of something.	• Something that is past its useful date.

2. **Take Your Pretest**
   Turn to the next page to the Pretest section and your teacher will ask you to write each list word one at a time.

Date: _____

Pretest – Lesson 28: Correction Area:

1. _____ _____
2. _____ _____
3. _____ _____
4. _____ _____
5. _____ _____
6. _____ _____
7. _____ _____
8. _____ _____
9. _____ _____
10. _____ _____
11. _____ _____
12. _____ _____
13. _____ _____
14. _____ _____
15. _____ _____
16. _____ _____
17. _____ _____
18. _____ _____

Carry-over Words: Correction Area:

1. _____ _____
2. _____ _____
3. _____ _____
4. _____ _____

Level 7, Lesson 28 – Words with **over** and **out**

Date: _____

Lesson 28
Day 2

carryover	leftover	bailout	outcome
discovered	overrated	cookout	checkout
governor	overcoat	devout	outgoing
controversy	recovery	outrageous	outdated
	takeover	outburst	

A. Read each clue. Write the list word in the blanks that answers each clue. **Unscramble** the highlighted rows to find the answer to the question asked. Write the answer to the question in the spaces provided.

1. Friendly.
2. Past its useful date.
3. Leader of a state.
4. A quarrel.
5. To rescue financially.
6. Outside cooking.
7. Devoted to religion.

(Unscramble the letters above to find the answer. Two letters have been filled in for you.)

"Raymond loved being the delivery boy for the pizza parlor, but when he asked his boss for a raise, all he got was the _____"

Answer: r __ __   __ __ o __ __ __

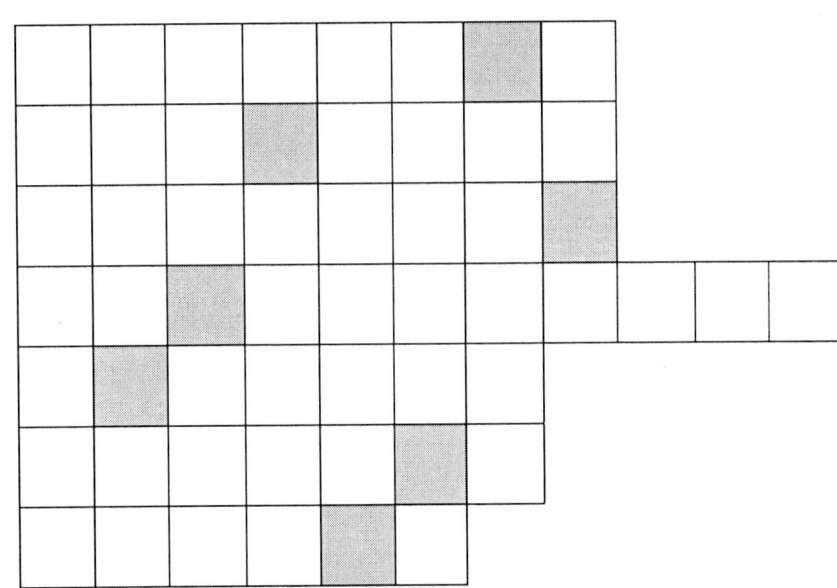

B. Write the definition from Day 1 for the list word **takeover**.

_____

_____

_____

_____

Level 7, Lesson 28 – Words with **over** and **out**

Lesson 28 Day 3

carryover	leftover	bailout	outcome
discovered	overrated	cookout	checkout
governor	overcoat	devout	outgoing
controversy	recovery	outrageous	outdated
	takeover	outburst	

A. Draw a line to connect each list word with its definition.

takeover	To assume or take control of something.
recovery	To regain normal heath.
overcoat	Something that is past its useful date.
overrated	Someone who is friendly and sociable.
leftover	Something that is extremely inappropriate.
carryover	One who is the top elected official of a state.
discovered	To rescue from financial difficulties.
governor	Someone who is devoted to religion.
controversy	To prepare food outdoors with a flame.
bailout	To place a value on something that is too high.
cookout	The result of something.
devout	A quarrel or disagreement.
outrageous	Food remaining from a meal.
outburst	The process of paying for goods.
outcome	A sudden blurting or loud noise from a human.
checkout	A sturdy garment worn over regular clothing.
outgoing	Something found for the first time.
outdated	Something brought forward.

B. Write a short paragraph below using at least four list words.

_____

_____

_____

_____

Level 7, Lesson 28 – Words with **over** and **out**

Date: _____

Lesson 28 Day 4

carryover	leftover	bailout	outcome
discovered	overrated	cookout	checkout
governor	overcoat	devout	outgoing
controversy	recovery	outrageous	outdated
	takeover	outburst	

A. Write the list words that match the dictionary pronunciations.

1. ʹkar-ē-ō-vər _____
2. ʹku̇k-oủt _____
3. oủt-ʹdāt-id _____
4. oủt-ʹrā-jəs _____
5. ʹtāk-ō-vər _____
6. ʹoủt-ˌkŭm _____
7. ʹoủt-bərst _____
8. ʹbāl-oủt _____
9. ʹoủt-gō-ing _____
10. ʹchek-oủt _____
11. di-ʹvoủt _____
12. ʹō-vər-kōt _____
13. ʹō-vər-ʹrāt-əd _____
14. ʹleft-ō-vər _____
15. ʹkȯn-trə-vər-sē _____
16. dis-kəv-ərd _____
17. rĭ-kŭv-ə-rē _____
18. ʹgŭv-ər-nər _____

B. Underline the correct words to complete the sentences.

1. The (governor, governer) passed the bill into law.
2. The judge warned everyone about making an (outberst, outburst) in court.
3. Angie was very (outgoeing, outgoing) and made friends with everyone.
4. Dad was tired of driving, so Mom agreed to (takeover, takieover) for while.
5. Emily suddenly (discovared, discovered) the underground cave.
6. Dad's necktie was fluorescent orange and clearly (outdaited, outdated).
7. We all love a good (cookout, coockout) on the grill.
8. The (outcome, outcom) of the contest was that the home team won the game.
9. We had a little (leftovar, leftover) pizza that Tony made on the grill.
10. After we gathered our food in the cart, it was time to (checkoute, checkout).

Level 7, Lesson 28 – Words with **over** and **out**

Date: _____

Lesson 28 - Day 5, Final Test

Correction Area:

1. _____
2. _____
3. _____
4. _____
5. _____
6. _____
7. _____
8. _____
9. _____
10. _____
11. _____
12. _____
13. _____
14. _____
15. _____
16. _____
17. _____
18. _____

Carry-over Words:

Correction Area:

1. _____
2. _____
3. _____
4. _____

Level 7, Lesson 28 – Words with **over** and **out**

Lesson 29 Day 1

Words with ei and ie

1. **Review Your List Words**
Look at the list words below and read each word to yourself. Then review each definition.

The general rule for **ei** and **ie** is **i** comes before **e** except after **c**. Of course, as you will see below, there are exceptions to this rule.

-The letter combination **ei** is often pronounced as one sound, such as in the words rec**ei**pt (**long e** sound), sl**ei**gh (**long a** sound), and h**ei**st (**long i** sound).

-The letter combination **ie** is often pronounced as one sound, such as in the words d**ie**sel (**long e** sound) and fr**ie**ndly (**short e** sound).

-The **ie** combination can also make different sounds, such as in the words **anxiety** and **glacier**.

List Words/Definitions

diesel — A fuel that is ignited by compression and heat created from an internal combustion engine.	**heightened** — To increase or make higher.
sleigh — A horse-drawn vehicle with skis for traveling over snow.	**anxiety** — Apprehension or fear of what might happen.
fiercest — Having a violent nature. Ferocious.	**weird** — Very unusual or strange.
friendly — Warm, kind, and comforting.	**eighteen** — One more than seventeen. Ten plus eight.
glacier — A large ice structure slowly flowing over a land mass.	**weightlifter** — One who uses weights to build strength or muscle mass.
receipt — Written proof of a purchase.	**freight** — Transported goods or cargo.
briefly — Something that lasts a short time.	**heist** — To rob or steal something.
unbelievable — To not accept as the truth.	**shriek** — A loud, sharp, verbal noise.
neighborhood — A place where people live close together as part of a community.	**foreigner** — One who is a not a citizen of the country in question.

2. **Take Your Pretest**
Turn to the next page to the Pretest section and your teacher will ask you to write each list word one at a time.

Level 7, Lesson 29 – Words with **ei** and **ie**

Date: _____

Pretest – Lesson 29:   Correction Area:

1. _____   _____
2. _____   _____
3. _____   _____
4. _____   _____
5. _____   _____
6. _____   _____
7. _____   _____
8. _____   _____
9. _____   _____
10. _____   _____
11. _____   _____
12. _____   _____
13. _____   _____
14. _____   _____
15. _____   _____
16. _____   _____
17. _____   _____
18. _____   _____

Carry-over Words: Correction Area:

1. _____   _____
2. _____   _____
3. _____   _____
4. _____   _____

Level 7, Lesson 29 – Words with **ei** and **ie**

Date: _____

Lesson 29 Day 2

diesel	glacier	heightened	freight
sleigh	receipt	anxiety	heist
fiercest	briefly	weird	shriek
friendly	unbelievable	eighteen	foreigner
	neighborhood	weightlifter	

A. Find and circle each list word in the puzzle below.

```
T V T A T L V X T U E N S B V
Y P Y E E S V S F N Y P L P J
D T H S H O E R Q B L E E C R
E R E R Y C T E R E F N I G D
O I I I R X S R E L E X G L I
D E G E X I R U N I I J H A H
K E I H W N F N G E R Z O C U
D F N B T R A H I V B W I I I
O S J E E E B W E A C S L E P
H F E I T O E W R B E Q X R C
Q G G G R H Q N O L T S I E H
N H H H E A G I F E E A I Y X
T F O R E T F I L T H G I E W
T O V A U F R I E N D L Y O G
D T P I E C E R N H I F X C G
```

B. Copy the following sentence. **The weightlifter that lived in my neighborhood could push the car an unbelievable distance.**

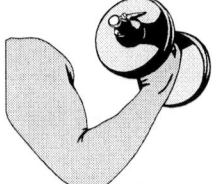

_____

_____

_____

_____

Level 7, Lesson 29 – Words with **ei** and **ie**

Date: _____

diesel	glacier	heightened	freight
sleigh	receipt	anxiety	heist
fiercest	briefly	weird	shriek
friendly	unbelievable	eighteen	foreigner
	neighborhood	weightlifter	

A. Write the list words as requested.

1. List words where the letter combination **ei** makes the long **a** sound.

   _____   _____

   _____   _____

   _____

2. List words where the letter combination **ie** or **ei** makes the long **e** sound.

   _____   _____

   _____   _____

   _____   _____

   _____

3. List words where the letter combination **ei** makes the long **i** sound.

   _____   _____

4. List words where the letter combination **ie** or **ei** makes the short **e** sound.

   _____   _____

5. List words where the letter combination **ie** makes **different** sounds.

   _____   _____

B. Write a short paragraph below using at least four list words.

_____

_____

_____

_____

Level 7, Lesson 29 – Words with **ei** and **ie**

Lesson 29 Day 4

diesel	glacier	heightened	freight
sleigh	receipt	anxiety	heist
fiercest	briefly	weird	shriek
friendly	unbelievable	eighteen	foreigner
	neighborhood	weightlifter	

A. Write a list word that matches each definition.

1. To rob or steal something.

2. To not accept as the truth.

3. One more than seventeen.

4. A loud, sharp, verbal noise.

5. Transported goods or cargo.

6. Something that lasts a short time.

7. Unusual or strange.

8. A horse-drawn vehicle with skis.

9. To increase or make higher.

10. Written proof of a purchase.

11. A large ice structure.

12. Fuel ignited by compression and heat.

13. Apprehension or fear.

14. One who uses weights to train.

15. Having a violent nature.

16. Warm, kind, and comforting.

17. A place where people live.

18. One who is a not a citizen of the country in question.

B. Write the definition from Day 1 for the list word **foreign**.

Level 7, Lesson 29 – Words with **ei** and **ie**

Date: _____

Lesson 29- Day 5, Final Test

Correction Area:

1. _____ _____
2. _____ _____
3. _____ _____
4. _____ _____
5. _____ _____
6. _____ _____
7. _____ _____
8. _____ _____
9. _____ _____
10. _____ _____
11. _____ _____
12. _____ _____
13. _____ _____
14. _____ _____
15. _____ _____
16. _____ _____
17. _____ _____
18. _____ _____

Carry-over Words:

Correction Area:

1. _____ _____
2. _____ _____
3. _____ _____
4. _____ _____

Level 7, Lesson 29 – Words with **ei** and **ie**

Date: _____

Lesson 30 Review Day 1

Review of words with silent letters

List Words

plumber	campaign	solemn	doughnut
raspberry	handsome	length	condemn
knowledge	gourmet	written	wreckage
knight	handkerchief	spaghetti	conscious
	rhythm	height	

A. Finish each list word.

1. _____um_____
2. _____ig_____
3. _____ow_____
4. _____yt_____
5. ___as_____
6. _____sc_____
7. ___ni_____
8. _____rm_____
9. _____pa_____
10. _____ds_____
11. _____ke_____
12. _____it_____
13. _____ug_____
14. ___pa_____
15. ___ol_____
16. _____ng_____
17. ___on_____n
18. _____ag___

B. Underline the correct words to complete the sentences.

1. The (handsome, handsom) (plummer, plumber) had a lot of (knowledge, knowlledge) in his head about fixing water leaks.

2. Fred had (written, ritten) a (solem, solemn) speech for his (campaign, campane).

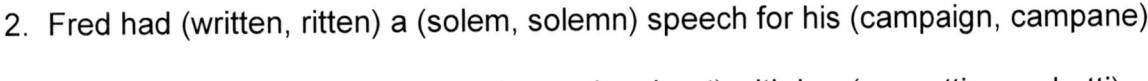

3. Joy ate a (razberry, raspberry) (donut, doughnut) with her (spagetti, spaghetti).

4. The small (lenth, length) of the (handkerchief, hankerchief) made a wave of (rythym, rhythm) when plucked.

5. The (conscious, consious) (nite, knight) was at quite a (hite, height) while sitting upon his horse.

6. State officials wanted to (comdem, condemn) the (reckage, wreckage) of the former (gormet, gourmet) restaurant.

Level 7, Lesson 30, Review of lessons 25-29

175

Lesson 30 Review Day 2

Review of easily misspelled words

List Words

changeable	hierarchy	minuscule	vacuum
discipline	inoculate	perseverance	definitely
exhilarate	maneuver	possession	congratulations
guarantee	medieval	questionnaire	liaison
	miniature	supersede	

A. Underline the list word in each group that is spelled correctly.

1. changeable — changable — changible
2. innoculate — inoculate — innoculaite
3. supercede — supersede — supurseed
4. guarantee — guarantie — guarenty
5. miniture — minature — miniature
6. leeason — liaison — liason
7. definitely — definetely — definately
8. vacume — vacuum — vacum
9. exhilerate — exhilarate — exhilerrate
10. manewver — maneauver — maneuver
11. discipline — disciplin — disciplan
12. medieval — midevil — midieval
13. congratudations — congratulations — congradulations
14. questionnaire — questionair — questionaire
15. minascule — minuscule — minnascule
16. higherarchy — hierarchy — hierarcy
17. posesion — possesion — possession
18. perserverance — perseverance — perservearance

B. Write a short paragraph below using at least four list words.

_____
_____
_____
_____

Level 7, Lesson 30, Review of lessons 25-29

Lesson 30 Review Day 3

Review of words with different **s** sounds

List Words

consider	simple	accuse	usual
disaster	insulate	residual	foreclosure
satisfy	usable	desire	visual
surrender	positive	measure	casual
	poison	pleasure	

A. Write each group of three list words in alphabetical order.

poison, pleasure, positive

1. _____   2. _____   3. _____

surrender, satisfy, simple

4. _____   5. _____   6. _____

consider, foreclosure, casual

7. _____   8. _____   9. _____

usual, usable, insulate

10. _____   11. _____   12. _____

casual, accuse, desire

13. _____   14. _____   15. _____

measure, visual, foreclosure

16. _____   17. _____   18. _____

surrender, residual, satisfy

19. _____   20. _____   21. _____

visual, positive, disaster

22. _____   23. _____   24. _____

simple, consider, satisfy

25. _____   26. _____   27. _____

Level 7, Lesson 30, Review of lessons 25-29

Lesson 30 Review Day 4

Date: _____

Review of words with **over** and **out**

List Words

carryover	leftover	bailout	outcome
discovered	overrated	cookout	checkout
governor	overcoat	devout	outgoing
controversy	recovery	outrageous	outdated
	takeover	outburst	

A. Finish the crossword puzzle.

Across:
1. Devoted to religion.
6. Remains from a meal.
9. Inappropriate or indecent.
11. To take control.
12. A result.
16. Past a usable date.
17. Brought forward from an earlier time or place.

Down:
2. Friendly or sociable.
3. Found for the first time.
4. A sudden loud noise.
5. Valued too high.
7. Head of a state.
8. Outdoor cooking.
10. To regain health.
13. To pay for goods.
14. To give financial assistance.
15. A dispute.
16. A heavy garment to keep warm.

Level 7, Lesson 30, Review of lessons 25-29

Lesson 30 Review Day 5

Review of words with ei and ie

List Words

diesel	glacier	heightened	freight
sleigh	receipt	anxiety	heist
fiercest	briefly	weird	shriek
friendly	unbelievable	eighteen	foreigner
	neighborhood	weightlifter	

A. Draw a line to connect each list word with its definition.

freight	One who is a not a citizen of the country in question.
heist	A place where people live as a community.
shriek	A loud sharp verbal noise.
foreigner	To not accept as the truth.
diesel	To rob or steal something.
sleigh	Something that lasts a short time.
fiercest	Transported goods or cargo.
friendly	Written proof of a purchase.
glacier	One more than seventeen.
receipt	Warm, kind, and comforting.
briefly	Having a violent nature.
unbelievable	One who uses weights to build strength.
neighborhood	A large ice structure that covers land.
heightened	Very unusual or strange.
anxiety	Fear of what might happen.
eighteen	A horse-drawn vehicle with skis.
weird	To increase or make higher.
weightlifter	A fuel that is ignited by a diesel engine.

Level 7, Lesson 30, Review of lessons 25-29

<<Intentionally left blank>>

Four-syllable words

1. **Review Your List Words**
Look at the list words below and read each word to yourself. Then review each definition.

Syllables are small units of sound that make up a word. When you have more than one syllable in a word, usually one of the syllables is more pronounced, which means it is emphasized more strongly, or loudly, than the other syllables.

Example: **combination**

This word has four syllables: **com**, **bi**, **na**, and **tion**. Notice that when you pronounce this word you naturally say it in four parts, **com-bi-na-tion**. You will also notice that the third syllable **na** is emphasized more than the other syllables.

List Words/Definitions

combination *combination*	redundancy *redundancy*
• A result from mixing two or more things together	• To have more than one; a duplicate.
alternative *alternative*	obliterate *obliterate*
• Another choice from what is offered.	• To remove or destroy something.
variety *variety*	stimulation *stimulation*
• Many different types of things.	• To arouse one's senses or awaken.
population *population*	medication *medication*
• The number of people who live in a town.	• Substances that are applied to or ingested into the body that have a healing quality.
absolutely *absolutely*	statutory *statutory*
• To be free from doubt.	• Something required by a law.
mandatory *mandatory*	identical *identical*
• Something that is required.	• To be exactly the same as something else.
conservative *conservative*	original *original*
• Cautious or traditional.	• The first one of something that has been duplicated.
exaggerate *exaggerate*	stupidity *stupidity*
• To inflate the truth beyond reality.	• The quality of lacking intelligence.
conspiracy *conspiracy*	intelligence *intelligence*
• A group of people who plan to do something that is sometimes illegal.	• Having the ability to learn and comprehend. To make sound decisions.

2. **Take Your Pretest**
Turn to the next page to the Pretest section and your teacher will ask you to write each list word one at a time.

Date: _____

Pretest – Lesson 31:

Correction Area:

1. _____   _____
2. _____   _____
3. _____   _____
4. _____   _____
5. _____   _____
6. _____   _____
7. _____   _____
8. _____   _____
9. _____   _____
10. _____   _____
11. _____   _____
12. _____   _____
13. _____   _____
14. _____   _____
15. _____   _____
16. _____   _____
17. _____   _____
18. _____   _____

Carry-over Words:

Correction Area:

1. _____   _____
2. _____   _____
3. _____   _____
4. _____   _____

Level 7, Lesson 31 – Four-syllable words

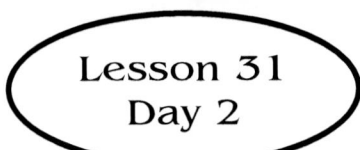

Lesson 31 Day 2

Date: _____

combination	absolutely	redundancy	identical
alternative	mandatory	obliterate	original
variety	conservative	stimulation	stupidity
population	exaggerate	medication	intelligence
	conspiracy	statutory	

A. The list words are all four-syllable words. Divide each list word into the syllables that make the word by writing each syllable on the lines. The first one has been done for you.

1. combination   __com__   __bi__   __na__   __tion__

2. absolutely   _____   _____   _____   _____

3. statutory   _____   _____   _____   _____

4. intelligence   _____   _____   _____   _____

5. population   _____   _____   _____   _____

6. variety   _____   _____   _____   _____

7. redundancy   _____   _____   _____   _____

8. identical   _____   _____   _____   _____

9. original   _____   _____   _____   _____

10. stimulation   _____   _____   _____   _____

11. medication   _____   _____   _____   _____

12. exaggerate   _____   _____   _____   _____

13. conservative   _____   _____   _____   _____

14. alternative   _____   _____   _____   _____

15. mandatory   _____   _____   _____   _____

16. conspiracy   _____   _____   _____   _____

17. obliterate   _____   _____   _____   _____

18. stupidity   _____   _____   _____   _____

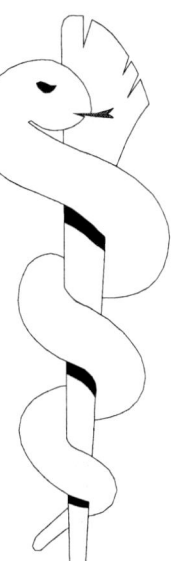

Level 7, Lesson 31 – Four-syllable words

Date: _____

combination	absolutely	redundancy	identical
alternative	mandatory	obliterate	original
variety	conservative	stimulation	stupidity
population	exaggerate	medication	intelligence
	conspiracy	statutory	

A. **Proofreading.** Underline any words that are misspelled. Insert **punctuation** where needed. Mark an **X** through any letters that are incorrectly **capitalized** or through any incorrect **punctuation**. **Circle** any letters that should be **capitalized** but are not. Correctly write the list words in the order they appear in the above paragraphs.

    the alterative to the mandtory Medicatian was, a combinaition of a veriaty of origenal plants administered by the conservitive doctor from the town with a small populatian? The effectiveness of the new drug was absolutuly identicle! to the old version and helped oblitarate the disease

1. _____ 2. _____ 3. _____

4. _____ 5. _____ 6. _____

7. _____ 8. _____ 9. _____

10. _____ 11. _____

    there was a conspirecy among! the thieves to exxagerate the effectiveness of the redundency of the burglar alarms at the bank. because of their stupididy they, tried to rob the bank and got caught   It was statatory that no one, especially with intelligance, or any stimualation of the brain for that matter, is Allowed to steal from the bank.

12. _____ 13. _____ 14. _____

15. _____ 16. _____ 17. _____

18. _____

B. Write the definition from Day 1 for the list word **intelligence**.

_____

_____

_____

_____

Level 7, Lesson 31 – Four-syllable words

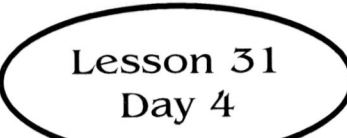

Lesson 31 Day 4

combination	absolutely	redundancy	identical
alternative	mandatory	obliterate	original
variety	conservative	stimulation	stupidity
population	exaggerate	medication	intelligence
	conspiracy	statutory	

A. Write the list words that match the dictionary pronunciations.

1. kŏm-bə-'nā-shən

2. man-də-,tōr-ē

3. pŏp-yə-'lā-shən

4. rĭ-'dŭn-dən-sē

5. və-'rī-ĭ-tē

6. kən-'sər-və-tĭv

7. stăch-ə-,tōr-ē

8. ĭn'těl-ə-jəns

9. stim-yə-'lā-shən

10. ə-rij-ə-nəl

11. med-ĭ-'kā-shən

12. ĭg-'zăj-ə-rāt

13. ól-'tər-nə-tĭv

14. ab-sə-lüt-lē

15. kən-'spir-ə-sē

16. ə-blĭt-ə-rāt

17. ī-'děn-tĭ-kəl

18. stú-pĭd-ĭ-tē

B. Copy the following sentence. **The red car that I purchased looked identical to the original car grandpa had many years ago.**

Level 7, Lesson 31 – Four-syllable words 185

Date: _____

Lesson 31 - Day 5, Final Test

Correction Area:

1. _____
2. _____
3. _____
4. _____
5. _____
6. _____
7. _____
8. _____
9. _____
10. _____
11. _____
12. _____
13. _____
14. _____
15. _____
16. _____
17. _____
18. _____

Carry-over Words:

Correction Area:

1. _____
2. _____
3. _____
4. _____

Level 7, Lesson 31 – Four-syllable words

Lesson 32 Day 1

Words with prefixes uni, mono, bi, tri, and mid

1. **Review Your List Words**
   Look at the list words below and read each word to yourself. Then review each definition.

   - The prefixes **mono** and **uni** mean **one**.
   - The prefix **tri** means three.
   - The prefix **bi** means **two**.
   - The prefix **mid** means in the middle.

List Words/Definitions

unilateral *unilateral*		**binoculars** *binoculars*	
• Involving the decision of only one person or side.		• A hand-held device used for viewing objects in the distance, which uses two separate telescopes.	
university *university*		**bipartisan** *bipartisan*	
• A place of higher learning such as a college. The students and faculty of one institution.		• Something that is supported by two different political parties.	
uniformity *uniformity*		**trilateral** *trilateral*	
• A condition where everything is exactly the same. Conforming to one standard.		• Something that involves three sides.	
monogram *monogram*		**trilogy** *trilogy*	
• A design consisting of letters (initials) printed as one symbol on objects.		• A set of three separate movies that tells a story.	
monopoly *monopoly*		**trimester** *trimester*	
• A market where there is only one seller of a good or services.		• A smaller unit of time that is one-third the size of the entire unit.	
monotone *monotone*		**triplicate** *triplicate*	
• A voice that has one tone.		• To reproduce something three times.	
monotonous *monotonous*		**middleman** *middleman*	
• Something that is boring and always repeated in one way.		• One who buys and sells goods, but not to the ultimate consumer.	
bilateral *bilateral*		**midpoint** *midpoint*	
• Something that involves two sides.		• A point that is exactly in the middle of two end points.	
bilingual *bilingual*		**midshipman** *midshipman*	
• Able to use two languages.		• A student naval officer. A middle, temporary rank.	

2. **Take Your Pretest**
   Turn to the next page to the Pretest section and your teacher will ask you to write each list word one at a time.

Level 7, Lesson 32 – Words with prefixes **uni**, **mono**, **bi**, **tri**, and **mid**

Date: _____

Pretest – Lesson 32: | Correction Area:

1. _____
2. _____
3. _____
4. _____
5. _____
6. _____
7. _____
8. _____
9. _____
10. _____
11. _____
12. _____
13. _____
14. _____
15. _____
16. _____
17. _____
18. _____

Carry-over Words: | Correction Area:

1. _____
2. _____
3. _____
4. _____

Level 7, Lesson 32 – Words with prefixes **uni**, **mono**, **bi**, **tri**, and **mid**

Lesson 32 Day 2

Date: _____

unilateral	monopoly	binoculars	triplicate
university	monotone	bipartisan	middleman
uniformity	monotonous	trilateral	midpoint
monogram	bilateral	trilogy	midshipman
	bilingual	trimester	

A. Finish the crossword puzzle.

Across:
3. Initials on a shirt.
4. Speaks two languages.
5. Concerns two sides.
7. Three movies.
8. Half way in between.
11. Concerns three sides.
13. Navy officer in training.
15. All being the same.
16. Concerns one person.
17. One tone only.

Down:
1. Handheld magnifiers.
2. Supported by two political parties.
3. Boring.
6. The only seller of something.
9. One third of the entire unit.
10. Three of something.
12. Higher learning.
14. Does not sell to the consumer.

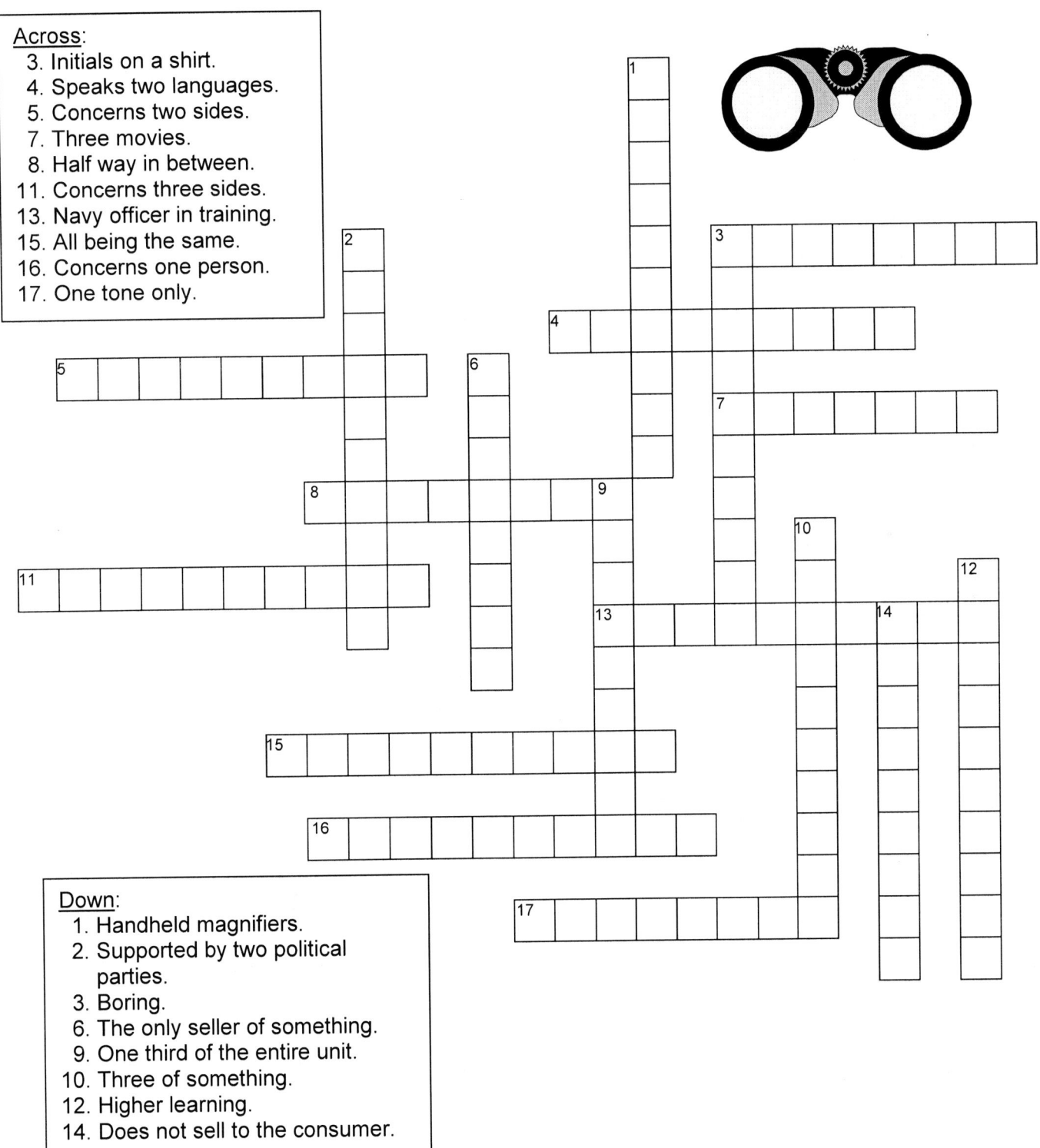

Level 7, Lesson 32 – Words with prefixes **uni**, **mono**, **bi**, **tri**, and **mid**

Lesson 32 Day 3

Date: _____

unilateral	monopoly	binoculars	triplicate
university	monotone	bipartisan	middleman
uniformity	monotonous	trilateral	midpoint
monogram	bilateral	trilogy	midshipman
	bilingual	trimester	

A. Write a list word that matches each definition.

1. Involves three sides.
   _____

2. One who does not sell to the consumer.
   _____

3. Condition where everything is the same.
   _____

4. A point that is exactly in the middle.
   _____

5. Three of something.
   _____

6. A student naval officer.
   _____

7. Supported by two political parties.
   _____

8. Speaks two languages.
   _____

9. A smaller unit that is one-third.
   _____

10. A voice that does not vary in pitch.
    _____

11. Something that involves two sides.
    _____

12. Initials on a shirt used as one design.
    _____

13. Involving only one person.
    _____

14. A place of higher learning.
    _____

15. Only one seller of goods.
    _____

16. Three movies that tell a story.
    _____

17. Boring and always the same.
    _____

18. A device for viewing at a distance.
    _____

B. Copy the following sentence. **The middleman sold binoculars to the university for their nature program.**

_____

_____

_____

Level 7, Lesson 32 – Words with prefixes **uni**, **mono**, **bi**, **tri**, and **mid**

Lesson 32 Day 4

unilateral	monopoly	binoculars	triplicate
university	monotone	bipartisan	middleman
uniformity	monotonous	trilateral	midpoint
monogram	bilateral	trilogy	midshipman
	bilingual	trimester	

Date: _____

A. Write the list word that completes each sentence.

1. _____ are often used to see things at a distance.
2. Darrel had a _____ of his initials sewed onto his shirt.
3. Patty was _____ in that she spoke Spanish and English.
4. Tom completed his second _____ of college.
5. The young soldier was a _____ on a submarine.
6. Tom had to fill out three copies of the application in _____.
7. Steve's Wholesale Stoves was a _____ for retailers.
8. The _____ agreement was between the three friends.
9. The _____ agreement was between Dan and his wife.
10. The _____ agreement allows Diane to make all the decisions.
11. There was _____ in the way the band members dressed.
12. Stan attended the _____ right after high school.
13. As the only seller of cowbells, you could say Randy had a _____.
14. My math professor lectured in a slow _____ voice.
15. Sitting in meetings day after day became _____.
16. The bill to implement new speed limits had _____ support.
17. We wanted to watch the entire _____ of the western story.
18. There was a gas station _____ between the store and home.

B. Write the definition from Day 1 for the list word **binoculars**.

_____

_____

_____

Level 7, Lesson 32 – Words with prefixes **uni**, **mono**, **bi**, **tri**, and **mid**

Lesson 32 - Day 5, Final Test

Date: _____

Correction Area:

1. _____   _____
2. _____   _____
3. _____   _____
4. _____   _____
5. _____   _____
6. _____   _____
7. _____   _____
8. _____   _____
9. _____   _____
10. _____   _____
11. _____   _____
12. _____   _____
13. _____   _____
14. _____   _____
15. _____   _____
16. _____   _____
17. _____   _____
18. _____   _____

Carry-over Words: **Correction Area:**

1. _____   _____
2. _____   _____
3. _____   _____
4. _____   _____

Level 7, Lesson 32 – Words with prefixes **uni**, **mono**, **bi**, **tri**, and **mid**

Date: _____

Words with sub, ultra, and dia

1. **Review Your List Words**
   Look at the list words below and read each word to yourself. Then review each definition.

List Words/Definitions

submarine *submarine*	diagram *diagram*
• A submersible water-going vessel.	• A drawing that shows interactions among variables.
substantial *substantial*	**diabolical** *diabolical*
• A large or significant amount.	• Something that is evil.
subsidize *subsidize*	**diagnose** *diagnose*
• To provide financial assistance.	• To recognize a disease by its symptoms.
subcontract *subcontract*	**dialect** *dialect*
• An agreement where someone else performs work for a contractor.	• A form of a language particular to a specific geographic region.
submission *submission*	**dialogue** *dialogue*
• The act of sending something for consideration.	• A conversation between people.
subpoena *subpoena*	**diatribe** *diatribe*
• A legal document commanding one to appear in court.	• A critical verbal attack on a person or idea.
ultrasonic *ultrasonic*	**subchapter** *subchapter*
• A device that has frequencies above those of audible sound. Often used for cleaning.	• A portion of a larger writing.
ultrasound *ultrasound*	**subcommittee** *subcommittee*
• High-frequency sound waves used to produce views of internal organs.	• A portion of a larger committee.
ultraviolet *ultraviolet*	**subjective** *subjective*
• Electromagnetic radiation with a wavelength shorter than that of visible light.	• A decision or liking that is an individual preference.

2. **Take Your Pretest**
   Turn to the next page to the Pretest section and your teacher will ask you to write each list word one at a time.

Date: _____

Pretest – Lesson 33:   Correction Area:

1. _____   _____
2. _____   _____
3. _____   _____
4. _____   _____
5. _____   _____
6. _____   _____
7. _____   _____
8. _____   _____
9. _____   _____
10. _____   _____
11. _____   _____
12. _____   _____
13. _____   _____
14. _____   _____
15. _____   _____
16. _____   _____
17. _____   _____
18. _____   _____

Carry-over Words: Correction Area:

1. _____   _____
2. _____   _____
3. _____   _____
4. _____   _____

Level 7, Lesson 33 – Words with **sub**, **ultra**, and **dia**

Lesson 33 Day 2

Date: _____

submarine	submission	diagram	diatribe
substantial	subpoena	diabolical	subchapter
subsidize	ultrasonic	diagnose	subcommittee
subcontract	ultrasound	dialect	subjective
	ultraviolet	dialogue	

A. Write each group of three list words in alphabetical order.

submarine, subcommittee, subjective

1. _____ 2. _____ 3. _____

diatribe, diagram, diabolical

4. _____ 5. _____ 6. _____

ultrasonic, ultrasound, ultraviolet

7. _____ 8. _____ 9. _____

subcommittee, subsidize, subchapter

10. _____ 11. _____ 12. _____

diagram, diatribe, dialogue

13. _____ 14. _____ 15. _____

subcontract, subchapter, submarine

16. _____ 17. _____ 18. _____

diabolical, diagnose, dialect

19. _____ 20. _____ 21. _____

substantial, submission, subpoena

22. _____ 23. _____ 24. _____

diagnose, dialogue, diagram

25. _____ 26. _____ 27. _____

subpoena, subchapter, subcommittee

28. _____ 29. _____ 30. _____

Level 7, Lesson 33 – Words with **sub**, **ultra**, and **dia**

Date: _____

Lesson 33 Day 3

submarine	submission	diagram	diatribe
substantial	subpoena	diabolical	subchapter
subsidize	ultrasonic	diagnose	subcommittee
subcontract	ultrasound	dialect	subjective
	ultraviolet	dialogue	

A. Find and circle each list word in the puzzle below.

```
U  L  T  R  A  S  O  U  N  D  W  I  P  X  X
L  M  O  S  U  B  P  O  E  N  A  K  I  H  C
T  L  A  C  I  L  O  B  A  I  D  E  R  I  E
R  L  E  R  L  S  R  Q  H  R  E  V  N  B  B
A  R  S  X  G  Q  U  X  B  T  J  O  S  S  I
V  E  O  U  G  A  G  B  T  P  S  F  U  E  R
I  T  N  Y  B  C  I  I  J  A  Z  B  B  K  T
O  P  G  E  B  C  M  D  R  E  M  P  M  E  A
L  A  A  F  E  M  O  T  R  I  C  B  A  K  I
E  H  I  M  O  O  L  N  S  L  Q  T  R  Z  D
T  C  D  C  S  U  B  S  T  A  N  T  I  A  L
R  B  B  C  P  M  I  N  D  R  B  I  N  V  H
D  U  E  U  G  O  L  A  I  D  A  O  E  Y  E
S  S  I  J  N  Z  D  I  A  L  E  C  T  H  L
E  Z  I  D  I  S  B  U  S  S  Y  O  T  S  K
```

B. Write the definition from Day 1 for the list word **dialogue**.

_____

_____

C. Write the definition from Day 1 for the list word **subsidize**.

_____

_____

Level 7, Lesson 33 – Words with **sub**, **ultra**, and **dia**

Date: _____

Lesson 33 Day 4

submarine	submission	diagram	diatribe
substantial	subpoena	diabolical	subchapter
subsidize	ultrasonic	diagnose	subcommittee
subcontract	ultrasound	dialect	subjective
	ultraviolet	dialogue	

A. Draw a line to connect each list word with its definition.

subjective — A legal document commanding one to appear.

subcommittee — A device that has frequencies above those of audible sound.

subchapter — Sound waves that produce views of organs.

diatribe — Something that is evil.

dialogue — A decision that is an individual preference.

dialect — To recognize a disease by its symptoms.

diagnose — The act of sending something for consideration.

diabolical — A submergible water going vessel.

diagram — Drawing that shows interactions among variables.

ultraviolet — A wavelength shorter than that of visible light.

ultrasound — A language particular to a specific region.

ultrasonic — A portion of a larger committee.

subpoena — To provide financial assistance.

submission — A conversation between people.

subcontract — A critical verbal attack on a person or idea.

subsidize — A portion of a larger writing.

substantial — One who performs work for a contractor.

submarine — A large or significant amount.

B. Cross out each word that is spelled incorrectly.

1. (submarine, submarene)
2. (substantial, substantal)
3. (subsidise, subsidize)
4. (subctrack, subcontract)
5. (submission, submision)
6. (subpena, subpoena)
7. (ultrasonnic, ultrasonic)
8. (ultraviolet, ultrvilet)
9. (digram, diagram)
10. (diabolical, dibolical)
11. (diagnoze, diagnose)
12. (dilect, dialect)
13. (dialogue, dialogg)
14. (ditribe, diatribe)
15. (ultrasound, ultrasond)
16. (subchaptr, subchapter)
17. (subcimitte, subcommittee)
18. (subjective, subjuctive)

Level 7, Lesson 33 – Words with **sub**, **ultra**, and **dia**

Lesson 33 - Day 5, Final Test

Correction Area:

1. _____
2. _____
3. _____
4. _____
5. _____
6. _____
7. _____
8. _____
9. _____
10. _____
11. _____
12. _____
13. _____
14. _____
15. _____
16. _____
17. _____
18. _____

Carry-over Words:

Correction Area:

1. _____
2. _____
3. _____
4. _____

Level 7, Lesson 33 – Words with **sub**, **ultra**, and **dia**

Lesson 34 Day 1

Words with **counter** and **super**

1. Review Your List Words
Look at the list words below and read each word to yourself. Then review each definition.

List Words/Definitions

Word	Definition
counteract *counteract*	To act against something so it will not continue on its own course.
counterattack *counterattack*	An attack against something that is already attacking.
counterclaim *counterclaim*	A retaliating lawsuit against a party who is already suing.
counterfeit *counterfeit*	Fake currency.
counteroffer *counteroffer*	An offer made in response to a previous offer.
supercenter *supercenter*	A retail store that is physically larger and has more selection than normal.
superficial *superficial*	Something that relates to the surface. Obvious.
superfluous *superfluous*	Exceeding what is required.
superglue *superglue*	An adhesive that has extra ordinary bonding powers.
superhero *superhero*	A mythical being that has extraordinary crime fighting abilities.
superimpose *superimpose*	To project or overlay an image on top of another image.
countermeasure *countermeasure*	A corrective action taken to offset a potentially harmful action.
counterproposal *counterproposal*	A response to a proposal.
superstitious *superstitious*	An unfounded fear of the unknown.
counterweight *counterweight*	A weight which counteracts the weight of another object.
supercar *supercar*	An automobile that has extreme performance capabilities.
superior *superior*	Something that is better compared to the others.
supermarket *supermarket*	A large food or retail store.

2. Take Your Pretest
Turn to the next page to the Pretest section and your teacher will ask you to write each list word one at a time.

Pretest - Lesson 34:

1. _____
2. _____
3. _____
4. _____
5. _____
6. _____
7. _____
8. _____
9. _____
10. _____
11. _____
12. _____
13. _____
14. _____
15. _____
16. _____
17. _____
18. _____

Correction Area:

_____
_____
_____
_____
_____
_____
_____
_____
_____
_____
_____
_____
_____
_____
_____
_____
_____
_____

Carry-over Words:

1. _____
2. _____
3. _____
4. _____

Correction Area:

_____
_____
_____
_____

Level 7, Lesson 34 – Words with **counter** and **super**

Date: _____

counteract	counteroffer	superimpose	counterweight
counterattack	supercenter	superhero	supercar
counterclaim	superficial	countermeasure	superior
counterfeit	superfluous	counterproposal	supermarket
	superglue	superstitious	

A. Read each clue. Write the list word in the blanks that answers each clue. **Unscramble** the highlighted rows to find the answer to the question asked. Write the answer to the question in the spaces provided.

1. A large food or retail store.
2. An act to disrupt the course of something.
3. Related to the surface.
4. Very strong glue.
5. Image on top of another.
6. Super crime fighter.
7. A very powerful car.
8. Better than the others.

(Unscramble the letters above to find the answer.)

"Curtis was glad to finally be the head electrician, but now he would be _____"

Answer: ___ ___   ___ ___ ___ ___ ___ ___

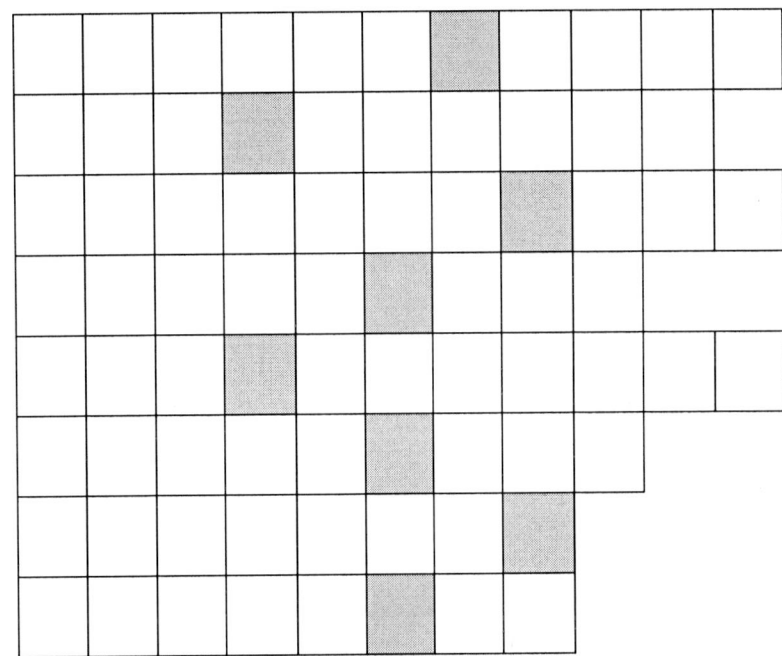

B. Write the definition from Day 1 for the list word **counteroffer**.

_____

_____

_____

C. Write the definition from Day 1 for the list word **superficial**.

_____

_____

_____

Level 7, Lesson 34 – Words with **counter** and **super**   201

Date: _____

Lesson 34 Day 3

counteract	counteroffer	superimpose	counterweight
counterattack	supercenter	superhero	supercar
counterclaim	superficial	countermeasure	superior
counterfeit	superfluous	counterproposal	supermarket
	superglue	superstitious	

A. Write each group of three list words in alphabetical order.

counterclaim, counterattack, counterfeit

1. _____ 2. _____ 3. _____

counteroffer, counterweight, counterproposal

4. _____ 5. _____ 6. _____

counteract, countermeasure, counteroffer

7. _____ 8. _____ 9. _____

superhero, superior, supermarket

10. _____ 11. _____ 12. _____

supercenter, superstitious, superfluous

13. _____ 14. _____ 15. _____

superficial, superfluous, superglue

16. _____ 17. _____ 18. _____

superimpose, supercar, superstitious

19. _____ 20. _____ 21. _____

superfluous, countermeasure, counterweight

22. _____ 23. _____ 24. _____

superior, supercenter, superficial

25. _____ 26. _____ 27. _____

superglue, superimpose, superstitious

28. _____ 29. _____ 30. _____

Level 7, Lesson 34 – Words with **counter** and **super**

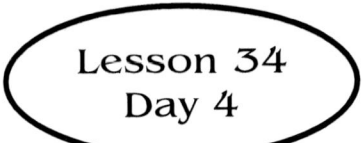

Date: _____

Lesson 34 Day 4

counteract	counteroffer	superimpose	counterweight
counterattack	supercenter	superhero	supercar
counterclaim	superficial	countermeasure	superior
counterfeit	superfluous	counterproposal	supermarket
	superglue	superstitious	

A. Finish each list word.

1. _____ct
2. _____ht
3. _____it
4. _____im
5. _____ce_____
6. _____ue
7. _____fi_____
8. _____or
9. _____pr_____
10. _____ma_____
11. _____fl_____
12. _____ca_____
13. _____ro_____
14. _____im_____
15. _____me_____
16. _____at_____
17. _____st_____
18. _____ro

B. Copy the following sentence. **The supermarket had a large assortment of superglue that was superior to the other store's glue because it could hold anything.**

_____
_____
_____
_____
_____

C. Copy the following sentence. **The countermeasure to their counterattack was superior, and the paintball game was won.**

_____
_____
_____
_____

Level 7, Lesson 34 – Words with **counter** and **super**

Lesson 34 - Day 5, Final Test

Correction Area:

1. _____
2. _____
3. _____
4. _____
5. _____
6. _____
7. _____
8. _____
9. _____
10. _____
11. _____
12. _____
13. _____
14. _____
15. _____
16. _____
17. _____
18. _____

Carry-over Words:

Correction Area:

1. _____
2. _____
3. _____
4. _____

Lesson 35 Day 1

Date: _____

Words that begin with consonant blends

1. **Review Your List Words**
Look at the list words below and read each word to yourself. Then review each definition.

A **consonant blend** is a group of two or more consonants that appear together in a word without any vowels between them. Each letter within the **blend** is pronounced individually.

The **consonant blend** in each word has been underlined.

List Words/Definitions

blockage *blockage*		**sl**umbered *slumbered*	
• Something that clogs or prevents the flow of something.		• To have slept.	
breakfast *breakfast*		**sk**eptical *skeptical*	
• The earliest meal of the morning.		• To be doubtful or cautious.	
dramatize *dramatize*		**squ**eaky *squeaky*	
• To present something in a dramatic or vivid manner.		• A sharp, high pitched sound.	
flattened *flattened*		**sm**army *smarmy*	
• To have been made thinner by crushing or pressure.		• The act of flattering another in an uncomfortable and excessive way.	
fragmented *fragmented*		**sn**orkel *snorkel*	
• To have broken something into many pieces.		• A breathing device that allows a swimmer's face to remain under water.	
glamorize *glamorize*		**sp**ecifically *specifically*	
• The act of making something appear attractive or desirable.		• Relating to a certain identified thing.	
grotesque *grotesque*		**st**ability *stability*	
• Very strange in appearance or manner. Disgusting.		• The condition of being reliable or secure.	
plebeian *plebeian*		**sw**elter *swelter*	
• A common person or one who is not upper class.		• To be extremely hot or humid.	
precarious *precarious*		**tr**emendous *tremendous*	
• Something that is not steady or stable.		• Something that is very large or excellent.	

2. **Take Your Pretest**
Turn to the next page to the Pretest section and your teacher will ask you to write each list word one at a time.

Level 7, Lesson 35 – Words that begin with **consonant blends**

Pretest – Lesson 35:   Correction Area:

1. _____   _____
2. _____   _____
3. _____   _____
4. _____   _____
5. _____   _____
6. _____   _____
7. _____   _____
8. _____   _____
9. _____   _____
10. _____   _____
11. _____   _____
12. _____   _____
13. _____   _____
14. _____   _____
15. _____   _____
16. _____   _____
17. _____   _____
18. _____   _____

Carry-over Words: Correction Area:

1. _____   _____
2. _____   _____
3. _____   _____
4. _____   _____

Level 7, Lesson 35 – Words that begin with **consonant blends**

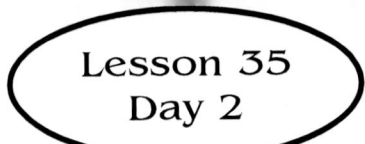

Lesson 35 Day 2

blockage	fragmented	slumbered	specifically
breakfast	glamorize	skeptical	stability
dramatize	grotesque	squeaky	swelter
flattened	plebeian	smarmy	tremendous
	precarious	snorkel	

A. Write the list word that completes each sentence.

1. The picture of the carnage after the hurricane was _____ to see.
2. Tony considered himself a common person; he was just a _____.
3. Stacie used a _____ when she watched fish underwater.
4. Bob would _____ in the hot garden if he stayed too long.
5. The _____ game show host flattered the contestants.
6. The newspapers will often _____ the movie stars.
7. The truck was teetering on the bridge in a _____ position.
8. Donald was _____ of the claims made by the sales clerk.
9. The children were a _____ help in doing the yard work.
10. Sandy and Paul would _____ their favorite scene from the play.
11. Curtis started every morning with a healthy _____.
12. Phyllis _____ soundly in her bed.
13. Alex _____ wanted that skateboard with the red stripes.
14. From his new job, Ben hoped to gain _____ and add to his savings.
15. The rusty old bicycle wheel was very _____ when it turned.
16. The beaver dam caused severe _____ in the river.
17. The broken dish had _____ into many pieces.
18. The can was _____ after it was run over by the car.

B. Write the definition from Day 1 for the list word **snorkel**.

_____
_____
_____
_____

Level 7, Lesson 35 – Words that begin with **consonant blends**   207

Date: _____

blockage	fragmented	slumbered	specifically
breakfast	glamorize	skeptical	stability
dramatize	grotesque	squeaky	swelter
flattened	plebeian	smarmy	tremendous
	precarious	snorkel	

A. Finish the crossword puzzle.

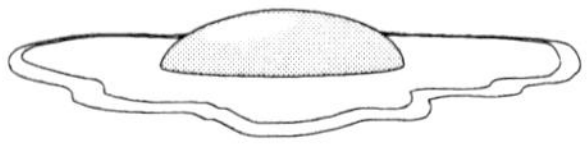

Across:
2. Broken into many pieces.
6. Unsteady.
9. Forced to be thinner.
10. Relating to an identified item.
11. Very hot.
12. To be doubtful.
13. Large or excellent.
15. Dependable.

Down:
1. Act out vividly.
3. To make desirable.
4. First meal of the day.
5. Strange in appearance.
7. Helps you breathe underwater.
8. Sleeping.
11. Flattering in an uncomfortable manner.
14. A common man.
15. High-pitched squeal.
16. A clog.

Level 7, Lesson 35 – Words that begin with **consonant blends**

Lesson 35 Day 4

blockage	fragmented	slumbered	specifically
breakfast	glamorize	skeptical	stability
dramatize	grotesque	squeaky	swelter
flattened	plebeian	smarmy	tremendous
	precarious	snorkel	

A. **Proofreading.** Underline any words that are misspelled. Insert **punctuation** where needed. Mark an **X** through any letters that are incorrectly **capitalized** or through any incorrect **punctuation**. **Circle** any letters that should be **capitalized** but are not. Correctly write the list words in the order in which they appear in the below paragraphs.

   barry was sceptical that it was specifcaly the sqeeky front wheel which let out a tromendous Noise as it flatened the plastic bottle The bottle fragented into a grotesk pile on the street. The rider lost his stabilite and was precarous for a minute.

1. _____   2. _____   3. _____
4. _____   5. _____   6. _____
7. _____   8. _____   9. _____

   after he slumberd and removed the blockiage from his ear. Mike the pleebian did not go outside to sweltr in the hot sun?   he ate brakefast and then sat down to watch the smarmey game show host drammitize the rules of the game as well as glammoriz fancy trips and prizes   One man actually won a snorkle trip

10. _____ 11. _____ 12. _____
13. _____ 14. _____ 15. _____
16. _____ 17. _____ 18. _____

B. Write a short paragraph below using at least four list words.

_____
_____
_____
_____
_____

Level 7, Lesson 35 – Words that begin with **consonant blends**

Lesson 35 - Day 5, Final Test

Correction Area:

1. _____
2. _____
3. _____
4. _____
5. _____
6. _____
7. _____
8. _____
9. _____
10. _____
11. _____
12. _____
13. _____
14. _____
15. _____
16. _____
17. _____
18. _____

Carry-over Words:

Correction Area:

1. _____
2. _____
3. _____
4. _____

Date: _____

Lesson 36 Review Day 1

Review of four-syllable words

List Words

combination	absolutely	redundancy	identical
alternative	mandatory	obliterate	original
variety	conservative	stimulation	stupidity
population	exaggerate	medication	intelligence
	conspiracy	statutory	

A. Find and circle each list word in the puzzle below.

Level 7, Review of lessons 31-35

Date: _____

Review of words with prefixes **uni**, **mono**, **bi**, **tri**, and **mid**

List Words

unilateral	monopoly	binoculars	triplicate
university	monotone	bipartisan	middleman
uniformity	monotonous	trilateral	midpoint
monogram	bilateral	trilogy	midshipman
	bilingual	trimester	

A. Read each clue. Write the list word in the blanks that answers each clue. **Unscramble** the highlighted rows to find the answer to the question asked. Write the answer to the question in the spaces provided.

1. Pertaining to one person.
2. Place of higher learning.
3. Only seller of something.
4. Pertaining to two people.
5. Speaks two languages.
6. Pertains to three people.
7. Three movies.
8. Does not sell to consumers

(Unscramble the letters above to find the answer.)

"Martha always wanted to be an operator at the telephone company, you could say it was _____."

Answer: h ___ ___   c ___ ___ ___ ___ ___ ___.

B. Write the definition from Day 1 for the list word **bipartisan**.

_____

_____

_____

Level 7, Review of lessons 31-35

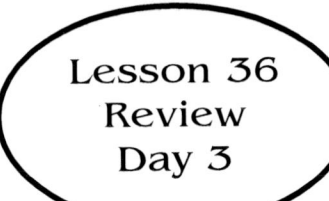

Lesson 36 Review Day 3

Review of words with **sub**, **ultra**, and **dia**

List Words

submarine	submission	diagram	diatribe
substantial	subpoena	diabolical	subchapter
subsidize	ultrasonic	diagnose	subcommittee
subcontract	ultrasound	dialect	subjective
	ultraviolet	dialogue	

A. Write the list word that completes each sentence.

1. The _____ dove way beneath the surface of the ocean.

2. The jewelry store used an _____ cleaner to clean the gold ring.

3. The _____ showed a view of Andrew's appendix.

4. The _____ light looked purple when plugged into the wall.

5. In this region of the country, the population has a distinctive _____.

6. Dr. Rawlins ran tests in order to _____ his patient's illness.

7. Ed was a member of a _____ as empowered by the full committee.

8. Alice agreed to _____ for the contractor of the construction job.

9. The government would _____ the cost of the student's rent.

10. The _____ showed the floor plans of the different stores.

11. After the _____ of his application, Chris got a loan at the bank.

12. The customer launched into an angry _____ at the sales clerk.

13. The specific _____ of the tax code was under main Chapter 12.

14. Whether or not you like something is said to be _____.

15. Craig and Wanda had a good _____ and spoke often.

16. The group had a _____ plan to rob the store.

17. The above group received a _____ from the court after being caught.

18. The above group also received a _____ amount of jail time.

Level 7, Review of lessons 31-35

Lesson 36 Review Day 4

Review of words with **counter** and **super**

Date: _____

List Words

counteract	counteroffer	superimpose	counterweight
counterattack	supercenter	superhero	supercar
counterclaim	superficial	countermeasure	superior
counterfeit	superfluous	counterproposal	supermarket
	superglue	superstitious	

A. Unscramble the following list words.

usperlgue

1. _____

uspermakret

2. _____

psuieror

3. _____

cuontrewgeiht

4. _____

spuefricial

5. _____

spucerenter

6. _____

cnoutoerffer

7. _____

conurtepproosal

8. _____

conuftereit

9. _____

conurteclmai

10. _____

conuettratack

11. _____

suepfrluuos

12. _____

sueprtsitious

13. _____

sruperca

14. _____

cotuentrac

15. _____

spuiermopse

16. _____

conuetrmaeseur

17. _____

seuprhoer

18. _____

Level 7, Review of lessons 31-35

Date: _____

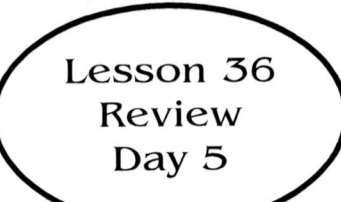

Lesson 36 Review Day 5

Review of words with **consonant blends**

List Words

blockage	fragmented	slumbered	specifically
breakfast	glamorize	skeptical	stability
dramatize	grotesque	squeaky	swelter
flattened	plebeian	smarmy	tremendous
	precarious	snorkel	

A. Write the list words that match the dictionary pronunciations.

1. ˈblŏ-kij _____
2. ˈglăm-ə-rīz _____
3. ˈslŭm-bərd _____
4. ˈskĕp-tĭ-kəl _____
5. spĕ-ˈsĭf-ĭk-ə-lē _____
6. stə-ˈbĭl-ĭ-tē _____
7. trĭ-ˈmĕn-dəs _____
8. ˈbrĕk-fəst _____
9. ˈdrăm-ə-tīz _____
10. ˈflăt-ənd _____
11. prĭ-ˈkĕr-ē-əs _____
12. plĭ-ˈbē-ən _____
13. ˈswĕl-tər _____
14. ˈfrăg-mənt-əd _____
15. ˈgrō-ˈtĕsk _____
16. ˈskwē-kē _____
17. ˈsmär-mē _____
18. ˈsnōr-kəl _____

B. Underline the correct words to complete the sentences.

1. The (blockage, blockege) in the pipe caused the sink to overflow.
2. It was a (tremendes, tremondous) honor to sit next to the president.
3. The terrible heat made the workers (swelter, sweltur) in the sun.
4. Dirk used a (snorkle, snorkel) to breath under the surface of the water.
5. One should never (glamorize, gamoriz) activities that are unhealthy.
6. The man was looking (specifically, specificly) for a watch as a present for his wife.
7. Sharon and Linda loved to (dramatise, dramatize) lines from funny moves.
8. Terrance (slumbered, slumberd) for most of the night.

Level 7, Review of lessons 31-35

<<Intentionally left blank>>